MATHEMATICS PLUS

HBJ

Harcourt Brace Jovanovich, Inc.

Orlando   Austin   San Diego   Chicago   Dallas   New York

Printed in the United States of America
ISBN 0-15-300137-2
2 3 4 5 6 7 8 9 10   030   95   94   93   92   91

PHOTOGRAPHERS

Table of Contents
iv, v, vi, HBJ/Earl Kogler; vii(t), HBJ/Jerry White; vii(b), vii, ix, x, HBJ/Earl Kogler

Introduction
xi, xii, xiii, xiv, HBJ/Earl Kogler

Chapter 1
1, HBJ/Britt Runion; 2(r), HBJ/Earl Kogler; 3, 5, Jim Bush; 6, HBJ/Earl Kogler; 15, 16, Jim Bush; 19, HBJ/Earl Kogler

Chapter 2
21, HBJ/Britt Runion; 22, HBJ/Earl Kogler; 25, 26, Jim Bush; 28, 31, 34(b), HBJ/Earl Kogler; 34(t), Jim Bush; 36(b), HBJ/Earl Kogler; 36(t), Jim Bush

Chapter 3
41, HBJ/Rob Downey; 43, 45, 47, 51, HBJ/Earl Kogler; 55, Jim Bush; 61, HBJ/Earl Kogler; 64, Larry Grant FPG

Chapter 4
67, HBJ/Rob Downey; 68(r), HBJ/Earl Kogler; 73(bc), Comstock; 73(bl), Pete Saloutos/The Stock Market; 73(br), Hanley & Savage/The Stock Market; 73(tc), R. Michael Stuckey/Comstock; 73(tl), Richard Hutchings/Photo Researchers; 73(tr), Janeart Ltd./The Image Bank; 75(bc), Sandy Roessler/The Stock Market; 75(bl), Comstock; 75(br), Superstock; 75(br), Superstock; 75(tc), Suzanne L. Murphy/FPG; 75(tl), Michael Phillip Manheim/The Stock Market; 75(tr), Roy Morsch/The Stock Market; 76, HBJ/Earl Kogler; 77, 79, 82, Jim Bush; 83, HBJ/Earl Kogler; 85, Jim Bush

Chapter 5
91, HBJ/Britt Runion; 93, HBJ/Earl Kogler; 101(b), Jim Bush; 101(t), HBJ/Earl Kogler; 102, Jim Bush; 107(l) (r), HBJ/J. White; 113, HBJ/Earl Kogler

Chapter 6
121, HBJ/Rob Downey; 122(l) (r), 127, HBJ/Earl Kogler; 130–132, Jim Bush

Chapter 7
141, HBJ/Rob Downey; 142, HBJ/Earl Kogler; 144, 148, Jim Bush; 149, HBJ/Earl Kogler; 151, 152, 154, Jim Bush; 159(bl) (br) (t), HBJ/Earl Kogler; 160, Jim Bush

Chapter 8
163, HBJ/Rob Downey; 164(l) (r), 165(bc) (bl) (br) (cc) (cl) (cr) (tc) (tl) (tr), 168(bl) (blc) (br) (brc) (tl) (tlc) (tr) (trc), HBJ/Earl Kogler; 169(all), HBJ/J. White; 175–185, 188, Jim Bush

Chapter 9
189, HBJ/Britt Runion; 190(l) (r), 191, HBJ/Earl Kogler; 193, HBJ/J. White; 195, 199, 200(b) (cb) (t) (tc), 203, 205(b) (t), HBJ/Earl Kogler

Chapter 10
207, HBJ/Britt Runion; 208, Jim Bush; 215, HBJ/Earl Kogler; 217, Jim Bush; 227, 228, HBJ/Earl Kogler; 229, 230, Jim Bush; 233, HBJ/Earl Kogler

Back Matter
All coins, Jim Bush

ILLUSTRATOR CREDITS

Angela Adams: 109, 110, 135(B), 136; **Lynn Adams:** 57, 58, 125, 126, 128(T), 221, 238A–238D; **Yvette Banek:** 4, 56, 66A-66D; **Bob Barner:** 3; **Lisa Berrett:** 49, 50, 240; **Carolyn Bracken:** 51, 52, 115 & 116 (flowers); **Olivia Cole:** 7, 8, 39, 40, 53, 54, 89, 90, 227, 228; **Roberta Collier:** 62; **Gwen Connelly:** 188A–188D; **Robbin Cuddy:** 67, 135(T), 145, 150, 174–176, 188, 195–196, 200, 211–212, 231–232, 235, 249, 250; **Fred Daunno:** 177–178, 219, 237–238; **Susanne DeMarco:** 23–24, 33, 35, 40A–40D, 119–120, 140A–140D, 166–167, 187, 207, 241–242, 251(M); **Nancy Didion:** 21; **Debbie Dieneman:** 47–48, 123–124; **Sharon Elzuardia:** 80–81; **Robert Frank:** 121; **Patrick Gnan:** 123 & 124 (backgrounds), 140; **Ethel Gold:** 2(BL), 29–30, 92; **Denny Hampson:** 9–10, 74; **Tonia Hampson:** 42, 65–66; **Pat Hinton:** 193–194; **Dennis Hockerman:** 97–98, 139, 141; **Anne Kennedy:** 162A–162D; **John Killgrew:** 5–6, 11–12, 18, 32, 55, 84(BL); **John Kurtz:** 1, 189; **Loretta Lustig:** 13–14, 59–60, 108, 133–134; **Tony Mascio:** 36; **Sal Murdocca;** 161, 223–224, 247; **Sherry Neidigh:** 27–28, 147, 153, 209–210, 225–226, 251(B), 253(T); **Sharron O'Neil:** 41, 63–64, 95–96, 103–104, 120A–120D, 215–216; **Sue Parnell:** 31, 78, 105–106, 131, 138(M), 163, 170, 186, 245; **Cathy Pavia:** 19–20, 43–44; **Robert Pennell:** 25, 61, 73, 75, 77, 84, 86, 102, 114 (background), 127–128, 142(BR), 146, 151, 155–158, 162, 173, 191–192, 203, 206, 220, 239, 246, 248; **Heidi Petach:** 99–100; **Tom Powers:** 71–72, 76, 83, 87–88; **Bob Shein:** 115 & 116 (windows), 143, 171–172; **Nancy Stevenson:** 20A–20D, 90A–90D; **Dorothy Stott:** 93–94, 111–112, 130; **Andrea Tachiero:** 91; **Lou Vaccaro:** 117–118, 129; **Joe Veno:** 17, 113–114, 233–234, 253(B); **Thelma Vroman:** 130 (T); **Tom Vroman:** 192(BR); **Justin Wager:** 197–198, 206A–206D; **John Wallner:** 45–46; **Jane Yamada:** 37–38, 69–70, 201–202, 204, 213–214, 222, 236, 243, 244(T), 257(M); **Lane Yerkes:** 137

Tim Bowers: M.C. Lion Mascot

AUTHORS

Grace M. Burton
Professor, Department of Curricular Studies
University of North Carolina at Wilmington
Wilmington, North Carolina

Jerome D. Kaplan
Professor of Education
Seton Hall University
South Orange, New Jersey

Martha H. Hopkins
Associate Professor
University of Central Florida
Orlando, Florida

Leonard Kennedy
Professor Emeritus
California State University at Sacramento
Sacramento, California

Howard C. Johnson
Chair, Mathematics Education
Professor of Mathematics and Mathematics Education
Syracuse University
Syracuse, New York

Karen A. Schultz
Professor, Mathematics Education
Georgia State University
Atlanta, Georgia

SENIOR EDITORIAL ADVISOR

Francis (Skip) Fennell
Professor of Education
Western Maryland College
Westminister, Maryland

ADVISORS

Janet S. Abbott
Curriculum Coordinator
Chula Vista Elementary School District
Chula Vista, California

Genevieve M. Knight
Professor of Mathematics
Coppin State College
Baltimore, Maryland

Steven Tipps
West Foundation Professor
Midwestern State University
Wichita Falls, Texas

Don S. Balka
Professor
Saint Mary's College
Notre Dame, Indiana

Charles Lamb
Associate Professor
University of Texas at Austin
Austin, Texas

David Wells
Retired Assistant Superintendent
for Instruction
Pontiac, Michigan

Gilbert Cuevas
Professor of Education
University of Miami
Miami, Florida

Marsha W. Lilly
Mathematics Coordinator, K–12
Alief Independent School District
Alief, Texas

Michael C. Hynes
Professor
University of Central Florida
Orlando, Florida

Sid Rachlin
Professor
University of Hawaii
Honolulu, Hawaii

▶ ▶ ▶ ▶ ▶ ▶ ▶ ▶

Contents ▶▶▶▶▶▶▶▶▶▶

INTRODUCING
◀ **Mathematics Plus** ▶

3   **Numbers 0 to 5   41**
    Theme • Fairy Tales and Nursery Rhymes

6 **Patterns** 121
   Theme • Seasons

▶▶▶▶▶▶▶▶▶▶▶▶▶▶▶▶

My Little Math Book

Home Note: Your child may enjoy reading this book to you.

1

Sorting and Counting

3

2

Shapes

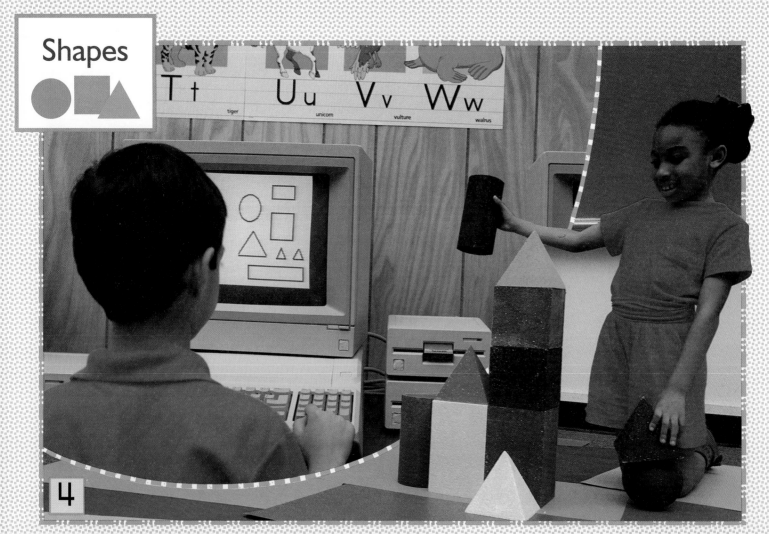

4

Patterns

5

✂

Measurement

7

Time and Money ⏰¢⏰¢⏰¢

6

🏠 School/Home Connection

Dear Family,
   I will be learning many new things in math this year. "My Little Math Book" shows ways I use math everyday, and the tools I will use to learn math.
   I will make a new "My Little Math Book" at the end of every chapter in my big math book. I can read these books to you all by myself.

                    Love,
                    Your child

8

Getting Ready

STORY TIME

Listen to the story.
"The Circus Clown"

School-Home Connection

Dear Family,
    Today we started Chapter 1 in our math book. We are learning about many new words in school. Some of the words are <u>top</u>, <u>middle</u>, <u>bottom</u>, <u>before</u>, <u>after</u>, <u>between</u>, <u>right</u>, <u>left</u>, <u>above</u>, <u>below</u>, <u>same</u>, and <u>different</u>. The activities below will help me understand how to use these words. Thanks for helping me.
                    Love,
                    Your child

Sharing and Doing

Bedroom

When your child is putting clothes away,
Ask: Which drawer are you using?
      (top, middle, bottom)
Say: Put socks in the top drawer.
      Put pants in the bottom drawer.
      Put shirts in the middle drawer.

Use after page 4.

Back Yard

Using a ball and a rope, have your child pass the ball to you above the rope and below the rope. When you pass the ball back, have your child tell whether you passed it above the rope or below it.

Use after page 8.

Place objects in monkeys' hands. **Top:** hat; **middle:** umbrella; **bottom:** banana. Remove objects and draw in place.

Home Note: Encourage your child to describe the picture, using the words *top*, *middle*, and *bottom*.

Shelves: Draw red ring around bottom; yellow ring around middle; blue ring around top.
Clown suit: Draw yellow X on middle button.

4

Identify positions and place circus cars as directed. Paste.

Home Note: Have your child describe the pictures, using the words *before, after,* and *between*.

5

6   Ring each child that is between.

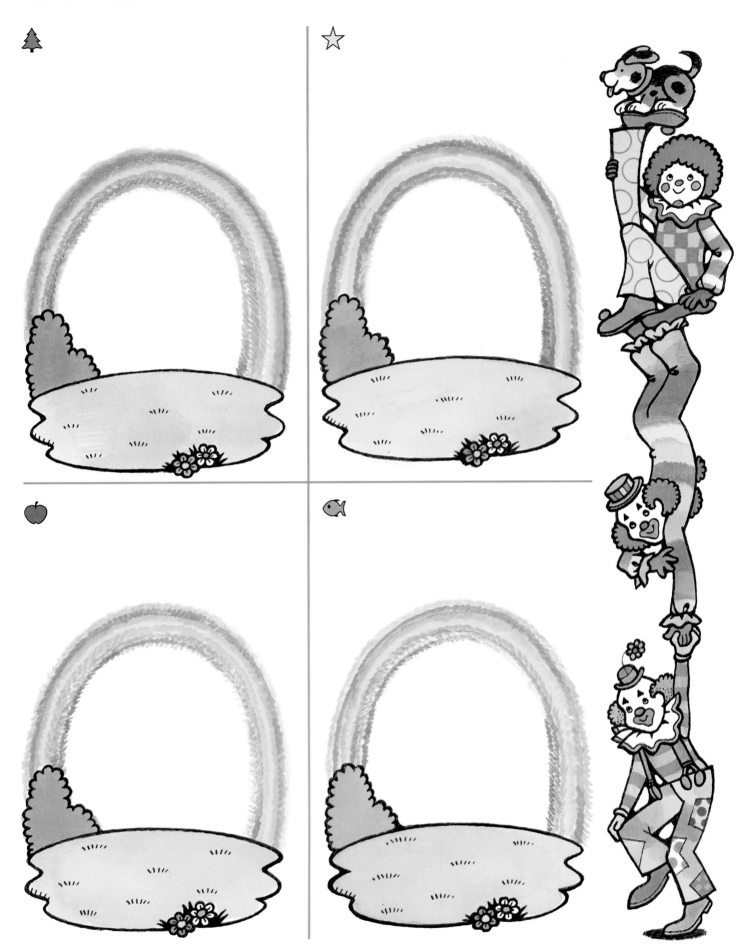

Tree: Put cloud above the rainbow. **Star:** Put gold below the rainbow. **Apple:** Put sun above the rainbow. **Fish:** Put cloud below the rainbow. Remove objects and draw in place.

Home Note: Encourage your child to discuss the pictures, using the words *above* and *below*.

7

Left: Color clothes above the belt red and below the belt blue. **Right:** Color the costume on the man that is above the other. Draw X on the object below the trapeze.

8

Left   Right

Put elephants on right. Put tigers on left.
Paste.

Home Note: Have your child describe the picture, using the words *right* and *left*.

9

Tree: Draw X on juggler at right. **Star:** Draw X on person at left. **Apple:** Draw X on person at left. **Fish:** Draw X on clown at right.

Color the clown to show the many ways he can dress.

Home Note: Have your child discuss the different ways the clown can dress.

Finish the Picture

Draw and color as directed.

Home Note: Encourage your child to discuss the things that were drawn in the picture.

Cut on lines. Sort in many ways.

14   Cut on lines. Sort by same and different.

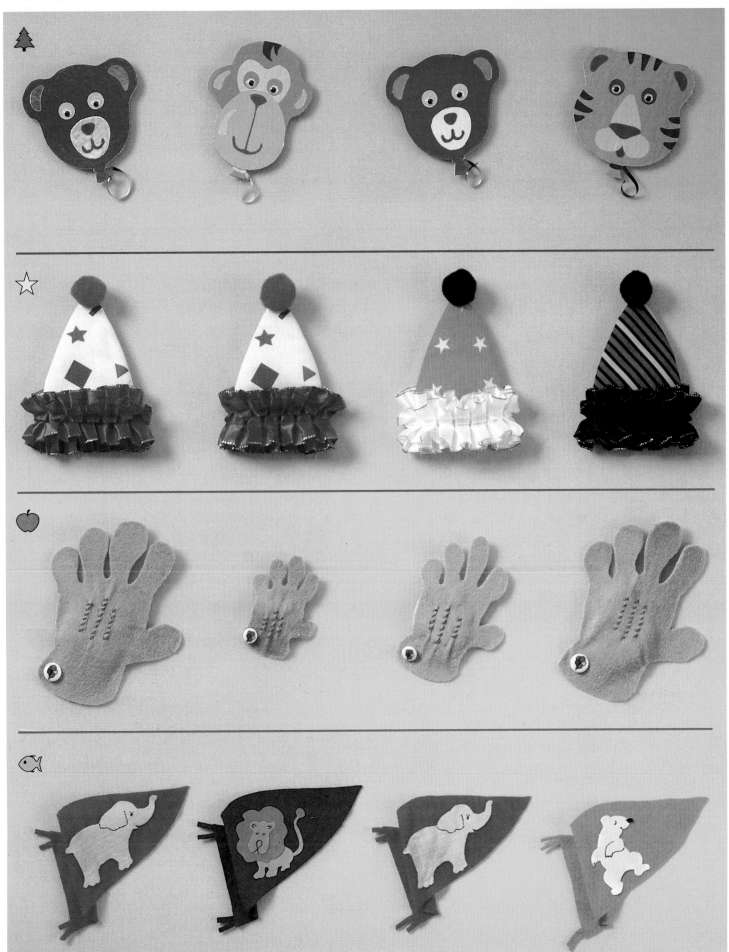

Draw a red ring around the objects in each row that are the same.

Home Note: Encourage your child to discuss the things in the pictures that are the *same* and the things that are *different*.

15

16   Draw a blue X on the object in each row that is different.

Find the circus flag that is the same. Color it
to match.

17

Chapter Review/Test

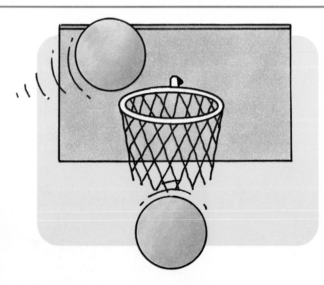

Draw rings and X's as directed.

Home Note: Have your child describe the pictures, using position words. Ask your child to find things that are the *same* and *different*.

A Day at the Circus

Describe the picture using words that tell where things are.

Home Note: Encourage your child to use words such as *above, below, between, before,* and *after.*

Draw rings around the things inside the circus ring. Draw X's on the things outside the circus ring.

Home Note: Have your child describe the picture, using the words *inside* and *outside*.

My Little Math Book

by _____

Home Note: Your child may enjoy reading this book to you. Encourage your child to use position words when pointing out people and objects on each page.

1

✂

Talk about the picture using the words before, after, and between.

3

2 Talk about the picture using the words top, middle, and bottom.

4 Talk about the picture using the words left and right.

Talk about the picture using the words above and below.

5

Talk about the picture using the words same and different.

7

6 Talk about the picture using the word same.

What do you see at this circus?

 Home Note: Talk about things that are the same and different. Identify the positions before, after, between, top, middle, and bottom.

8

CHAPTER 2

Sorting and Classifying

STORY TIME

Listen to the story.
"The Bake Sale"

BAKE SALE

Theme • Neighborhood **21**

School-Home Connection

Dear Family,
  Today we started Chapter 2 in our math book. We are learning to sort things by color and size. Here are some activities for us to do together at home.
        Love,
        Your child

Sharing and Doing

Kitchen

After the dishes and silverware have been washed and dried, have your child group all the similar pieces together. For example: all forks, then spoons, then plates, and so on. Then have your child put the silverware away.

Laundry Area

Before doing the wash, ask your child to help you sort the clothes into loads. Separate the light-colored clothes from the dark-colored clothes. After the laundry has been sorted, have your child tell whether each group has dark or light clothes. When the laundry is dry, have your child sort the socks into pairs.

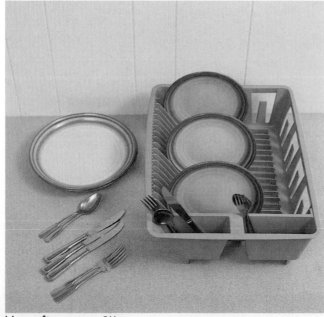

Use after page 24.

Use after page 24.

Sort by color. Put one color in each window.
Remove and color the flowerpots.

Home Note: Have your child explain how the
pots were sorted.

Draw a line the color of the star from each star to each object of the same color.

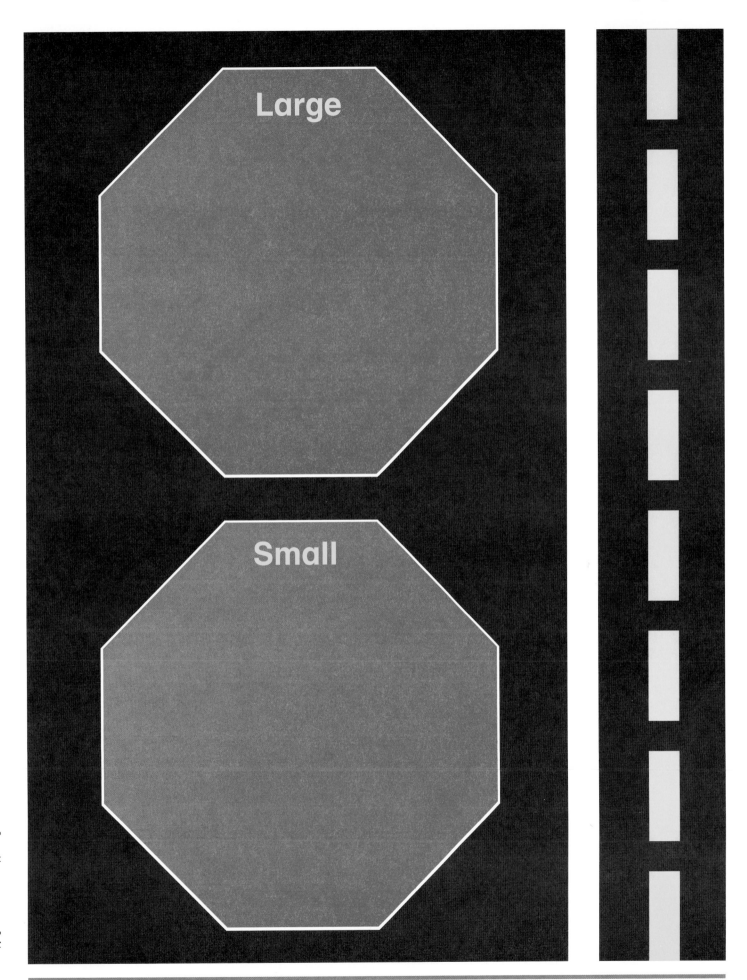

Large

Small

Sort by size. Put the large objects in the top
stop sign and the small objects in the
bottom stop sign.

Home Note: Have your child explain how the
vehicles were sorted.

25

26 Draw a line from large objects to the large star and from small objects to the small star.

Sort the bears. Put one group in each bus. Paste.

Home Note: Have your child explain how the bears were sorted.

Sort the clothes. Put one group on each clothesline, and paste.

Listen to the clues. Draw a ring.

Home Note: Encourage your child to create clues about a picture and have you guess the person, place, or object.

29

Which Path?

Start

Draw a line from the dog to the doghouse.

Put red windows in the building on the left. Have your friend put the same number of blue windows in the building on the right. Repeat. Then draw the windows and match.

Home Note: Have your child explain how groups of the same number were made.

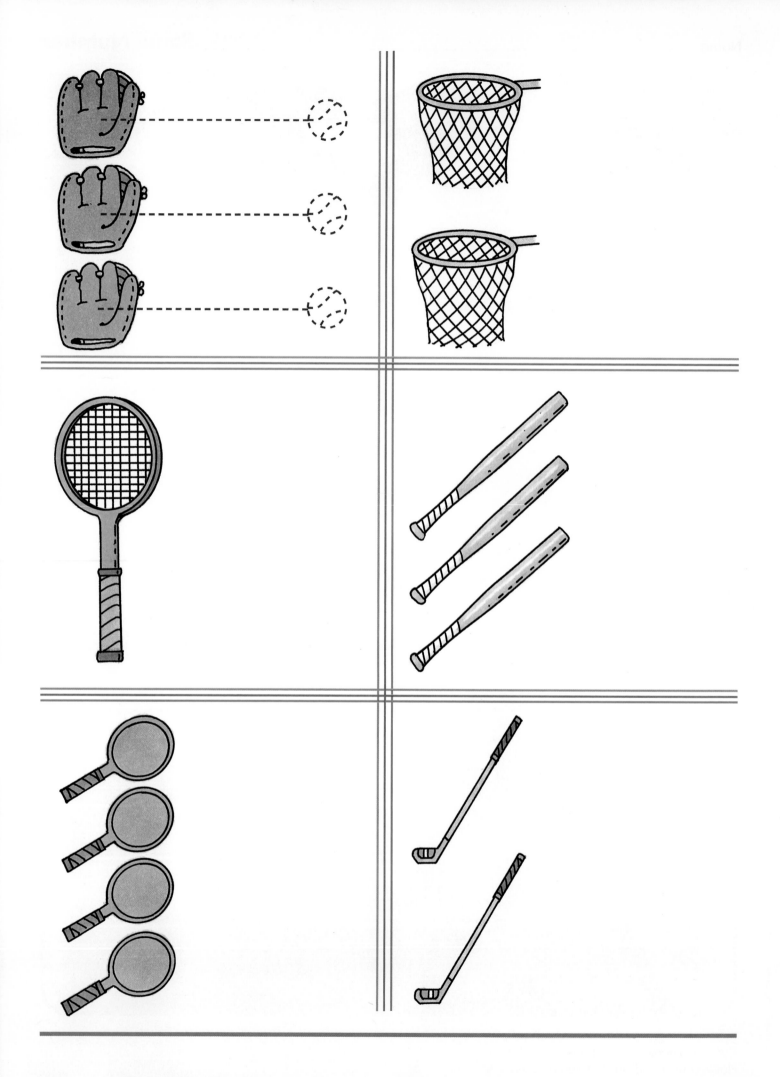

Draw a ball for each object. Then draw lines
to match the ball to the object.

More

Draw lines to match one object to another.
Ring the group that has more.

Home Note: Have your child explain which groups have more.

33

Use a blue crayon to draw a button to match each red button. Then draw more blue buttons.

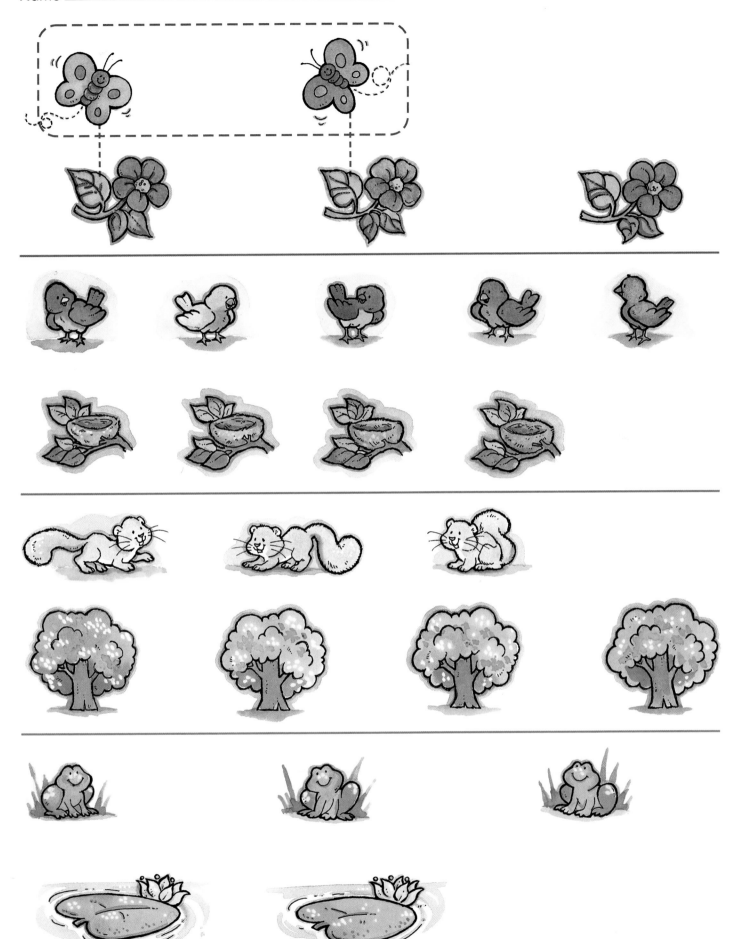

Draw lines to match one object to another.
Ring the group that has fewer.

Home Note: Have your child explain which groups have fewer.

Use a blue crayon to draw a row of fewer
buttons in each group.

Name _____

Put the fruit in the trees. Move the fruit to the graph. Paste. Ring the line on the graph that has more.

Home Note: Make a group of four things. Ask your child first to make a group with more and then to make a group with fewer.

37

Name _____

Top: Ring objects that are the same color. **Middle:** Draw X's on the objects that are the same size. **Bottom:** Use a green crayon to draw a group that has more buttons. Ring the group that has fewer.

9

Name _____

The Post Office

Talk about the things that are done at the post office.

Home Note: Have your child discuss the picture. Talk about how things are sorted at a post office. You may wish to give your child some empty mail envelopes to sort.

39

Name _____

A Day at the Park

Top: Draw something you might find at a playground. **Bottom:** Draw something you might have at a picnic.

40

My Little Math Book

by _____

Home Note: Your child may enjoy reading this book to you. Encourage your child to talk about each picture.

1

Home Note: Talk about how objects have been sorted.

3

  Home Note: Talk about how the clothes are being sorted.

More  or ?

Ring the group with more.

Nurse's Station

Ring the group with fewer.

5

Draw lines to match.

7

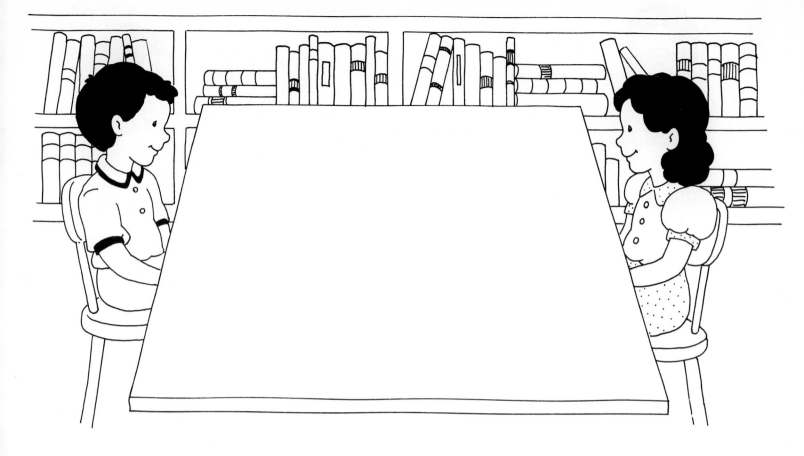

6 Draw a book for each child.

 Home Note: Talk about the picture. Find the groups with more or fewer. Find things that are the same.

STORY TIME

Listen to the story.
**"The Counting
Zoo"**

School-Home Connection

Dear Family,
  Today we started Chapter 3 in our math book. We will be learning about the numbers 0 to 5 and the positions first through fifth. Here's a game my teacher thought we might like to play at home.
            Love,
            Your child

Sharing and Doing

Penny Toss

Make a gameboard on a large piece of paper, as shown, or on the unmarked side of a large paper bag. Give each player a penny or a small stone.

Players take turns tossing the penny onto the gameboard. After the penny lands, the player reads the number it landed on. If the penny landed on a line or did not land on the gameboard, the player may toss again. The winner of each toss is the player whose penny lands on the greatest number.
Variations:
  1. Let the winner of each toss be the player whose penny lands on the least number, on the 3, or on any number you choose.
  2. Move farther away from the gameboard to make the game harder.

        HAVE FUN!

Use after page 54.

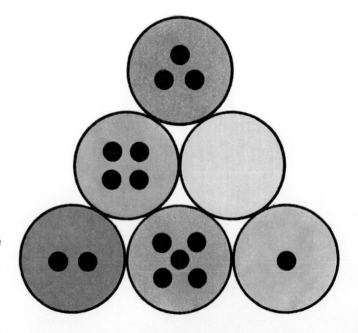

I

one

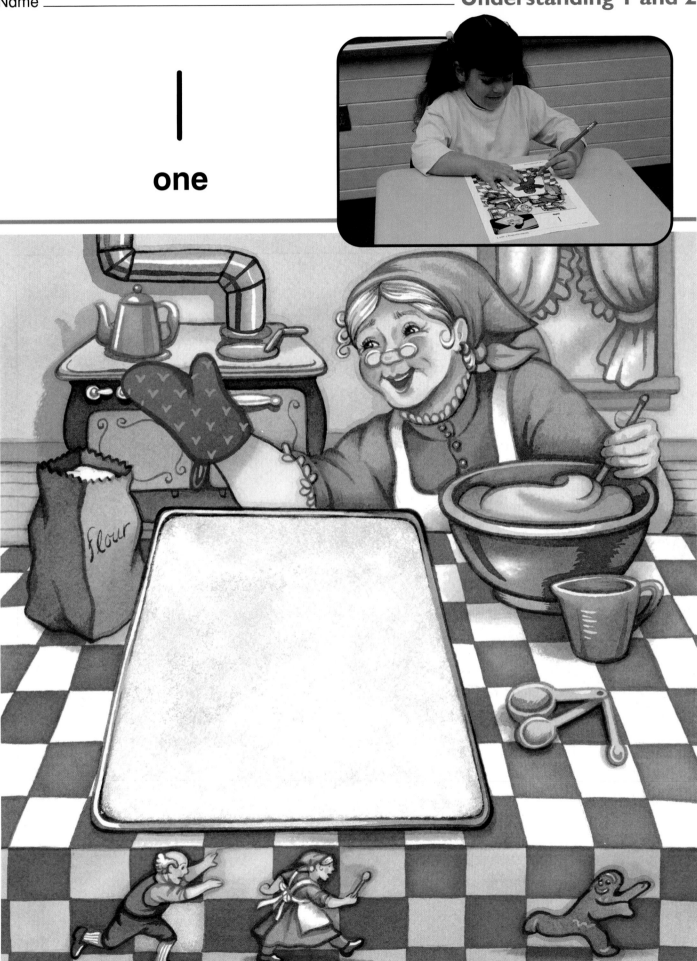

Show 1 gingerbread man. Trace.

Home Note: Have your child retell the story. Point out various objects at home of which there is only 1.

43

2 two

Top: Show 1. Trace. Show 1 more to make a group of 2. Trace. **Bottom:** Draw 1 cookie on the cookie sheet on the left. Draw 2 cookies on the cookie sheet on the right.

Pet Store

Put 1 counter on each puppy. Count the counters in each window. Ring each window that has 2 puppies.

Home Note: Encourage your child to point out objects in the home of which there are 1 or 2.

45

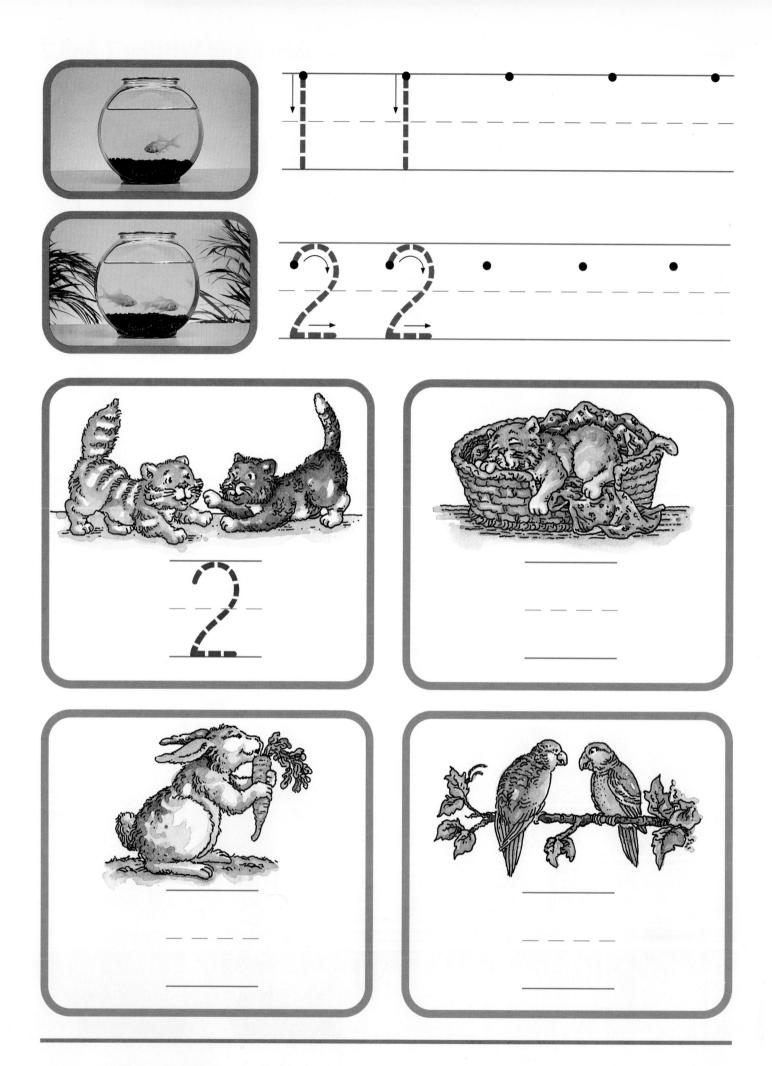

Top: Write ones and twos. **Bottom:** Count each animal. Write the number.

3
three

Top : Make a group of 2 on the rug. Trace.
Show 1 more to make a group of 3. Trace.
Bottom: Draw 3 bowls for porridge on the
table.

Home Note: Encourage your child to retell
the story of "The Three Bears." Then make
groups of 3 objects.

47

4 four

Top: Make a group of 3 on the rug. Show 1 more to make a group of 4. **Bottom:** Draw a group of 4 hats on the shelves.

Name _____   **Counting and Writing 3 and 4**

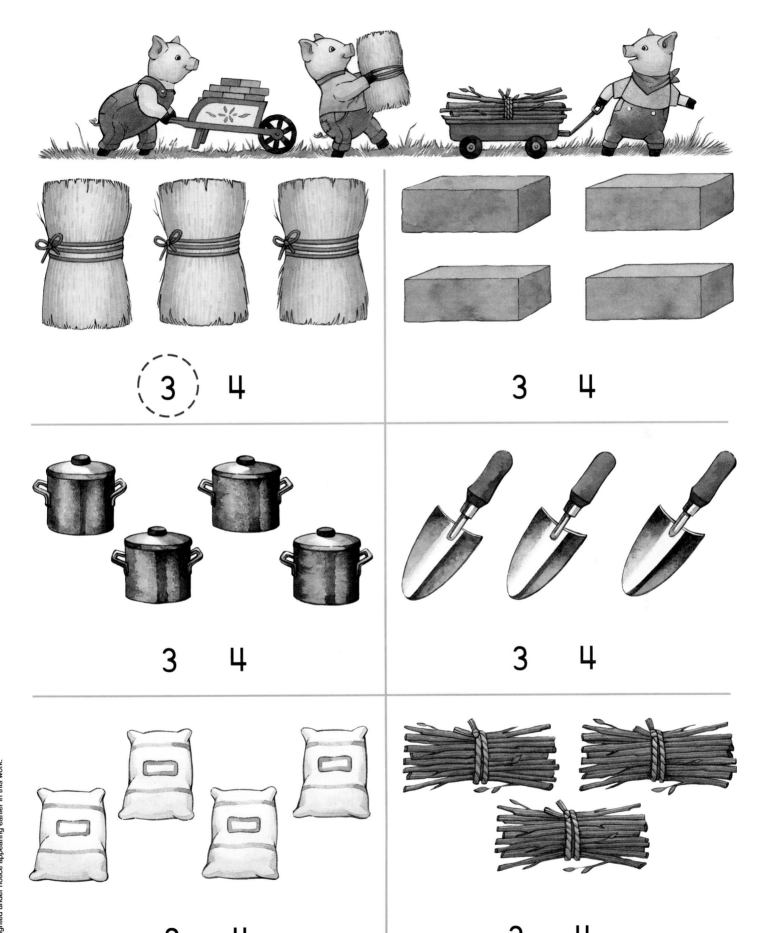

3   4

3   4

3   4

3   4

3   4

3   4

Place a counter on each object in the group. Count. Ring the correct number.

Home Note: Encourage your child to retell the story. Find groups of 3 and 4 objects.

49

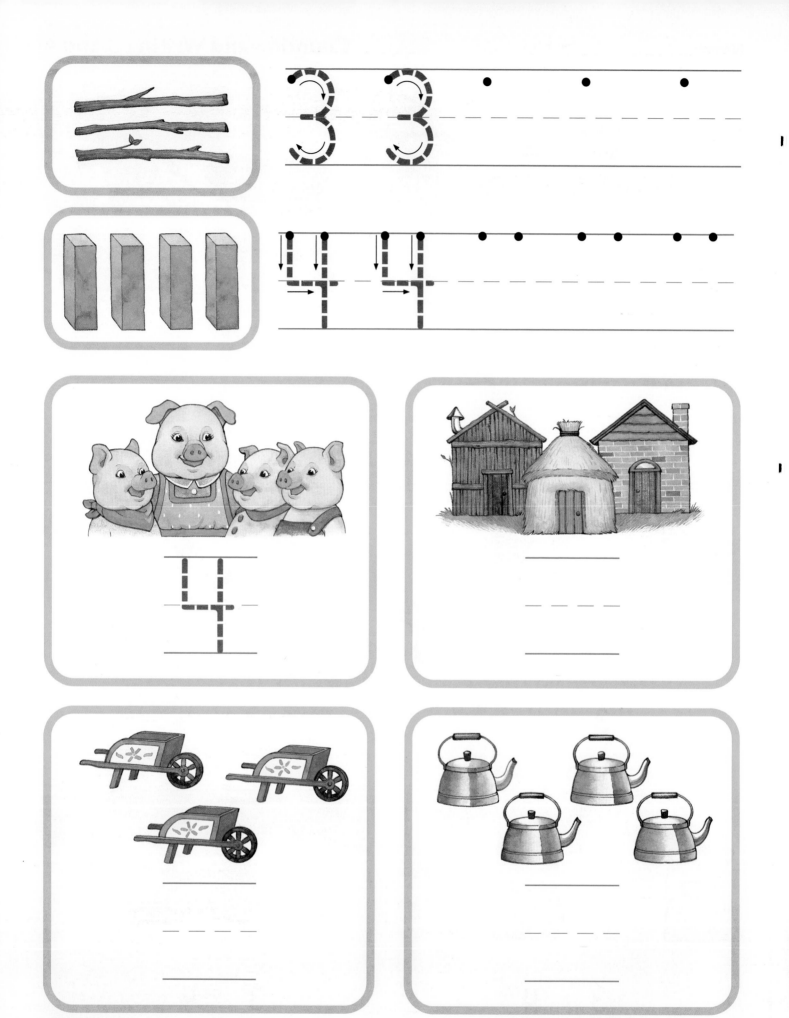

50

5
five

Place 4 flowers in the garden. Then place 1 more to make a group of 5. Remove and draw 5 flowers in the garden.

 Home Note: Encourage your child to make and count groups of 5 objects or fewer.

O zero

Top: Put flowers in the garden. Count them. Take them out. Show 0 flowers.

Bottom: Ring each vase that has 0 flowers.

52

How many ?

0   (5)

How many ?

0   5

How many ?

0   5

How many ?

0   5

Use your counters. Count. Ring the correct number.

Home Note: Have your child retell the story. Find objects that show 0. Find groups of 5.

53

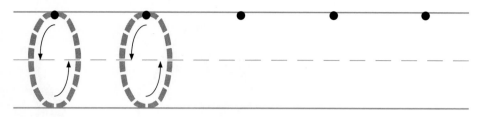

Top: Count. Write zeros and fives.
Bottom: Use the picture to tell how
many. Write the number.

54

Use your counters to count the objects in the picture. Color one box for each.

Home Note: Encourage your child to point out why the boxes are colored as they are.

Hidden Numbers

Top: Find and trace the numbers.
Bottom: Write the numbers.

Count the objects on the left. Write how many. Use your punchouts to put an equal number of objects on the right. Paste. Write the number.

Home Note: Encourage your child to talk about how the groups with an equal number were made.

57

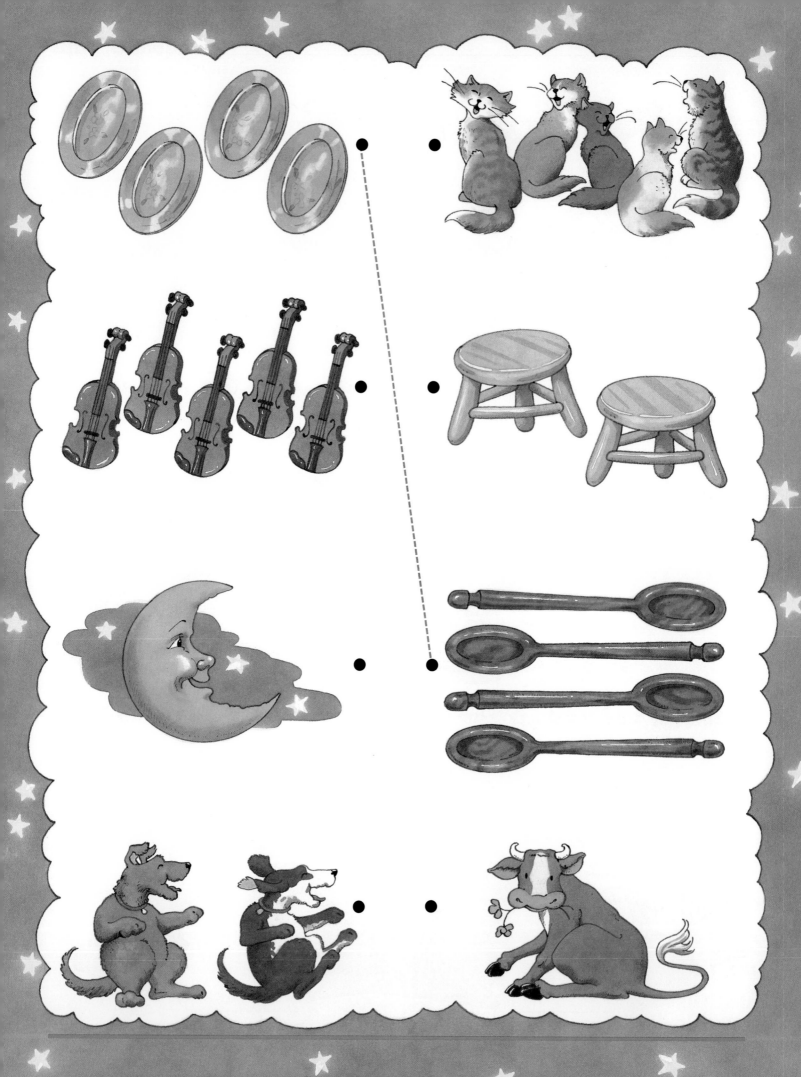

Count the objects in each group. Draw a line
between equal groups.

0
1
2
3
4
5

Draw and color the correct number of apples in each basket.

Home Note: Encourage your child to tell the order in which the apples were placed in the baskets.

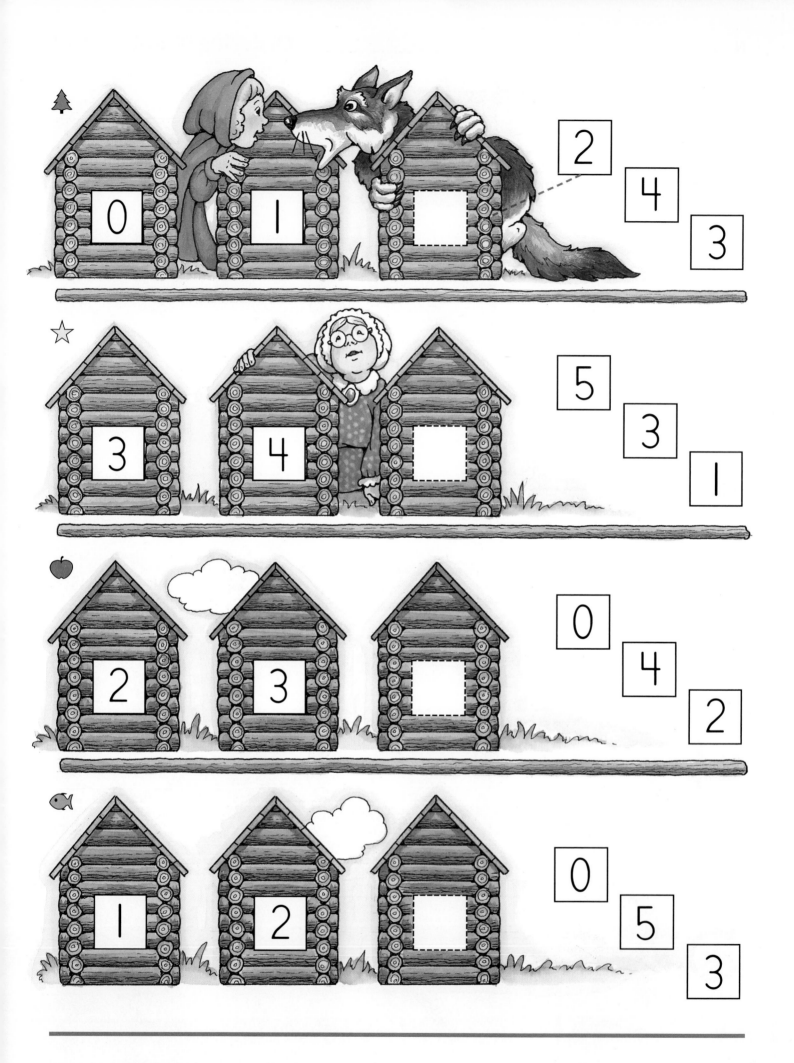

0 1 ☐   2 4 3

3 4 ☐   5 3 1

2 3 ☐   0 4 2

1 2 ☐   0 5 3

Look at the numbers on the houses. Draw a line to the number that comes next.

Put the toys on the steps. Doll: third step;
dog: fifth step; phone: first step; dinosaur:
fourth step.

Home Note: Have your child describe the
position of each toy.

Top: Ring the first; draw X on third.
Middle: Ring the second; draw X on fourth.
Bottom: Ring the fifth; draw X on third.

62

Name _____

Look at the picture. Write how many bunnies are wearing each color shirt.

Home Note: Encourage your child to retell the story. Then have your child explain how he or she knew what number to write by each color shirt.

63

Name _____

Chapter Review/Test

_____
- - - - -
_____

_____
- - - - -
_____

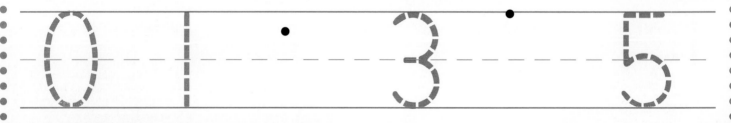

0   1   3   5

Top: Write the number in each group. Then match equal groups. **Middle:** Ring the second child. Draw X on fourth child. **Bottom:** Write the numbers 0 to 5 in order.

64

Chapter 3

Talk about "Old King Cole." Count the number of objects in each group. Compare the groups. Ring the groups with more than 3 objects.

Home Note: Encourage your child to retell the story. Practice counting groups of objects at home. Have your child identify groups as having more than or less than 3.

65

5   2   _____   _____

_____   _____   _____   _____

_____   _____   _____   _____

STORY TIME

Listen to the story.
"The Juggling Show"

School-Home Connection

Dear Family,
    Today we started Chapter 4 in our math book. We will be learning about shapes. We will also be learning about equal parts of shapes. Here are some activities my teacher thought we could have fun with at home.
                    Love,
                    Your child

Sharing and Doing

Kitchen

Help your child list all the shapes the two of you can find in the kitchen. Be sure to write both the object and the shape (example: oven doors are rectangles, toaster is shaped like a box). See how long you can make your list. See if another family member can make a longer list.

Kitchen

Encourage your child to show you one half of various objects in the kitchen such as a napkin, a loaf of bread, a sandwich, and so on.

Nam_____ **Ball, Box, Can, and Cone**

Draw a red ring around each box. Draw a green ring around each can. Draw a blue ring around each ball. Draw a yellow ring around each cone.

Home Note: Encourage your child to use the words *ball*, *box*, *can*, and *cone* to talk about the shapes of the objects.

69

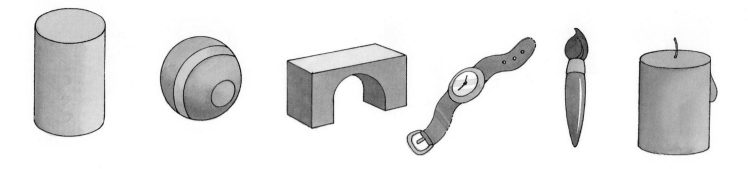

  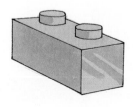  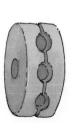 

Tree: Ring the objects shaped like a can.
Star: Ring the objects shaped like a box.
70 **Apple:** Ring the objects shaped like a ball.
Fish: Ring the objects shaped like a cone.

Ball

Box

Can

Cone

Sort the groceries by shape. Put them in the bag that has the same shape. Paste.

Home Note: Encourage your child to explain how the shapes are alike and how they are all different.

Ball

Box

Can

Cone

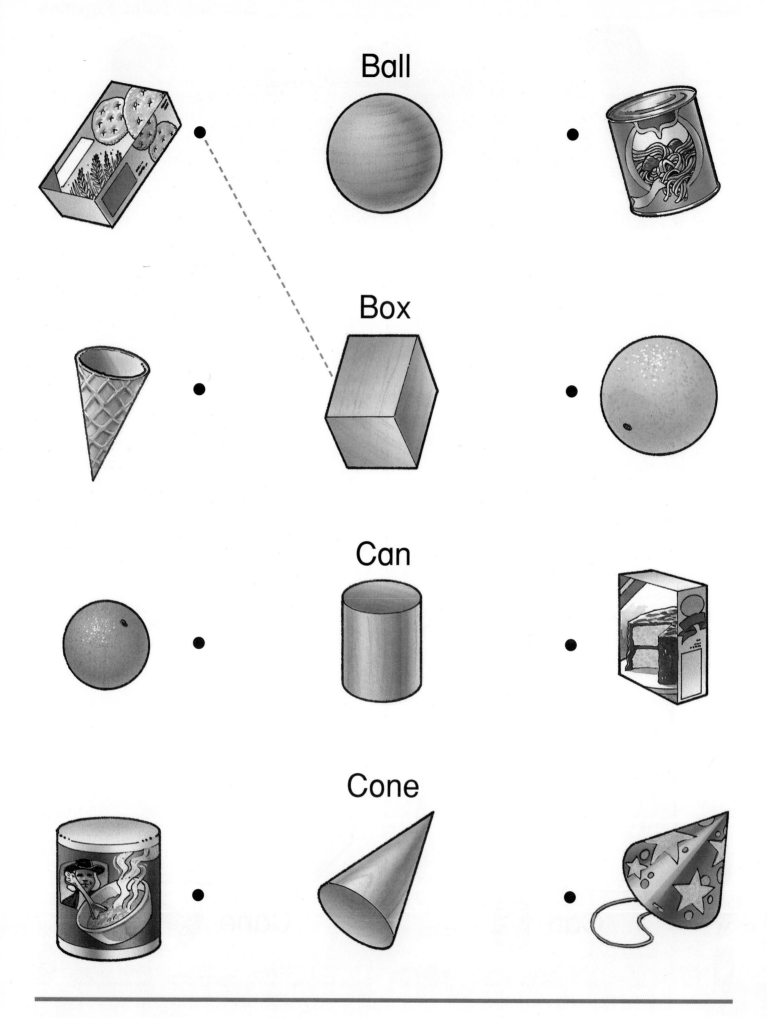

Draw a line from each object to the matching shape.

Circle

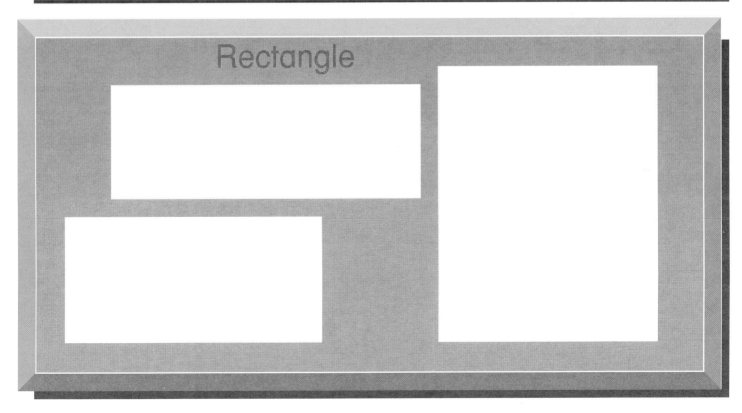

Rectangle

Sort the shapes. **Top:** Put each circle in the frame. **Bottom:** Put each rectangle in the frame. Paste.

Home Note: Encourage your child to explain why the pictures are placed as they are.

73

74

Top: Ring the objects shaped like circles.
Bottom: Ring the objects shaped like rectangles.

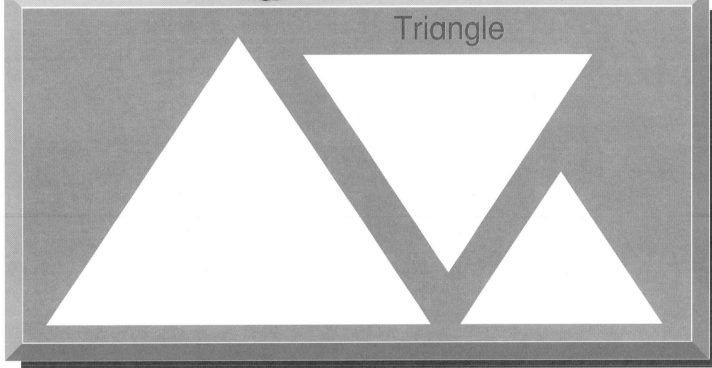

Triangle

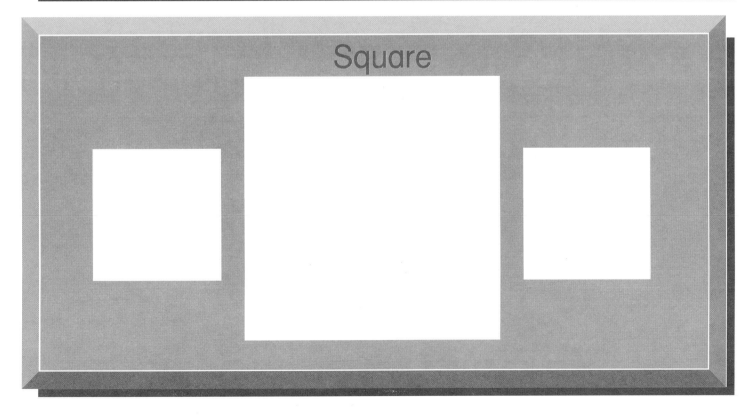

Square

Sort the shapes. **Top:** Put each triangle in the frame. **Bottom:** Put each square in the frame. Paste.

Home Note: Encourage your child to explain why the pictures are placed as they are.

75

Left: Color inside the triangles.
Right: Color inside the squares.

Name _____

Guesses will vary.

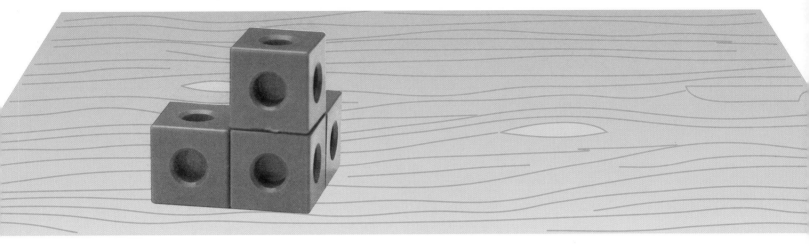

My Guess

How many?

My Guess

How many?

Guess how many blocks. Write the number.
Use blocks to make the design. Write the
number. Check your guess.

Home Note: Make some block designs.
Encourage your child to guess the number
of blocks in each and model the design.

77

Shape Art

How many?

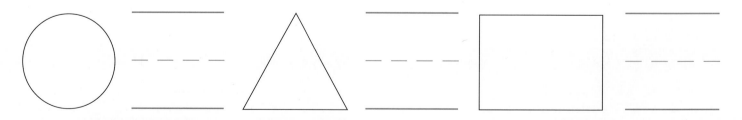

Find each shape. Color inside it. Count how many of each shape you colored. Write the number.

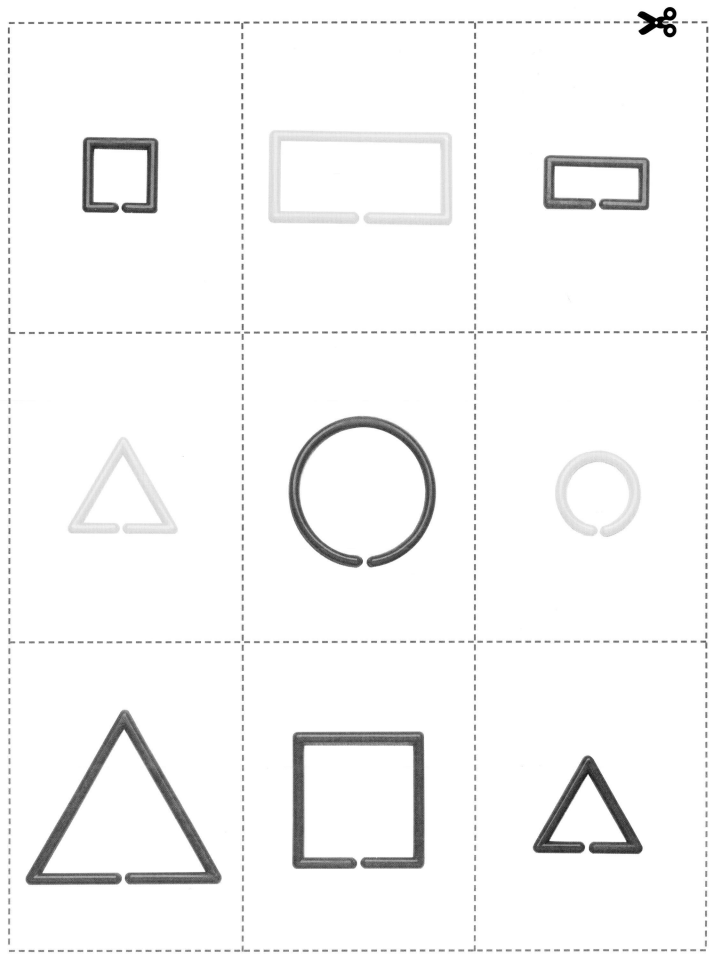

Sort and classify by more than one attribute.

Sort the objects.

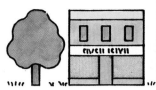

Large Square Village

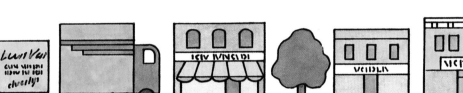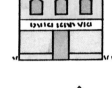

Small Blue Village

Sort the shapes. Put the shapes where they belong. Then trace the shapes and color.

Home Note: Encourage your child to explain how the shapes were sorted.

81

82 Draw a red ring around all the large red shapes.
Draw a blue ring around all the blue triangles.

Ring the sandwiches that show equal parts. Draw X on sandwiches that do not show fair shares, or equal parts.

Home Note: Have your child explain how to tell whether pieces of things are *equal*.

83

Ring the shapes that show equal parts.
Draw X on the shapes that do not show
equal parts.

84

Ring the fruit in each row that shows halves.

Home Note: Encourage your child to point out objects at home that show *halves*.

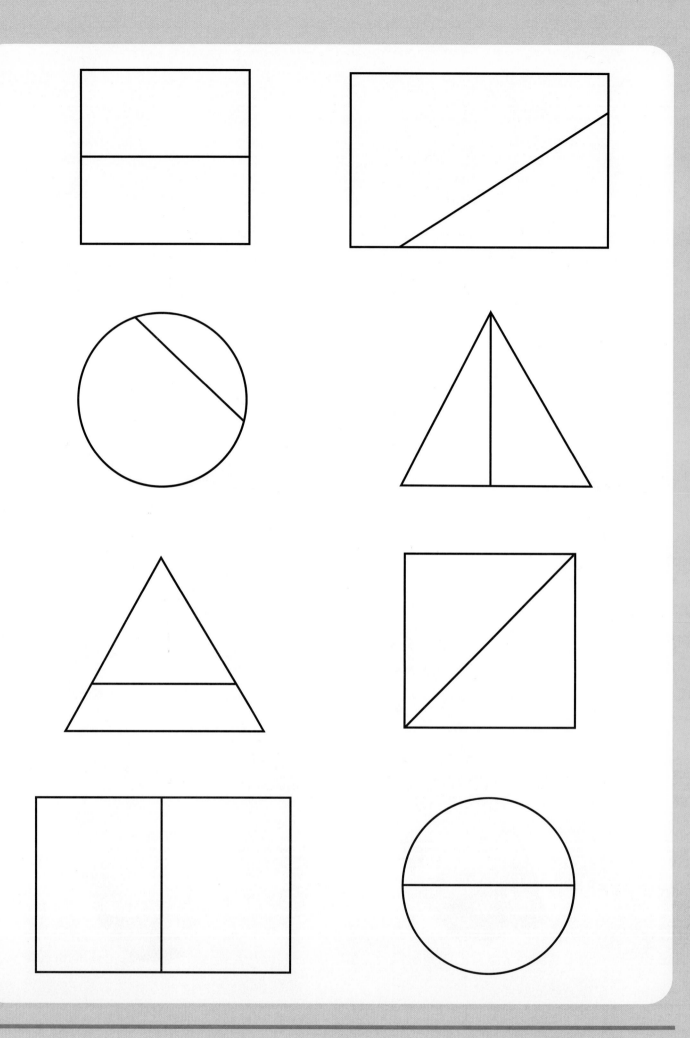

Ring the shapes that show halves. Color one half.

Find a pattern in the path. Then draw a line
to show the way from school to home.

Home Note: Encourage your child to talk
about the different shapes. Then have your
child point out the pattern.

87

Chapter Review/Test

🌲

⭐

🍎

🐟

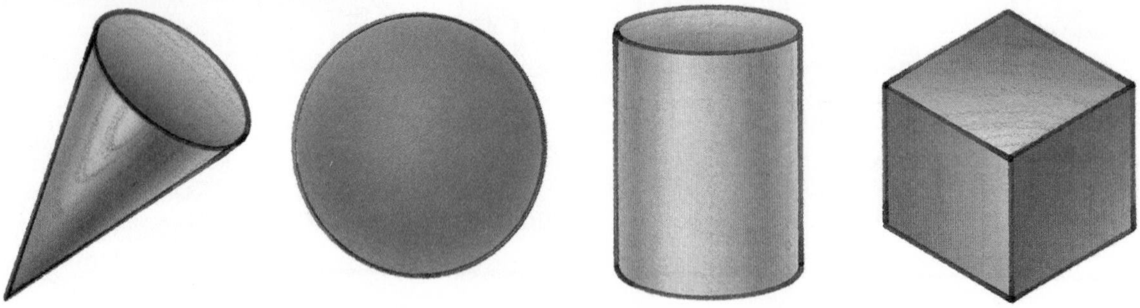

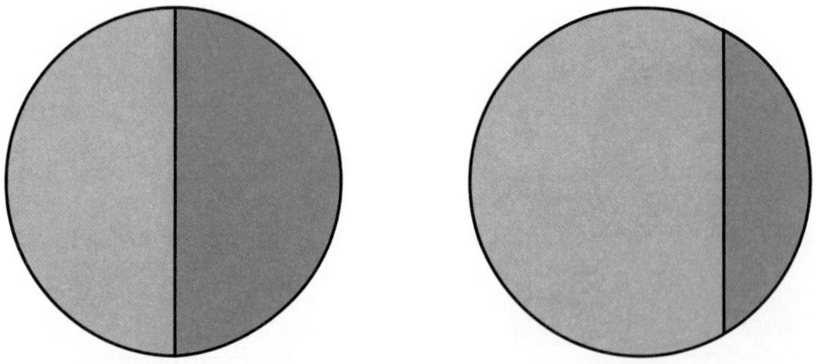

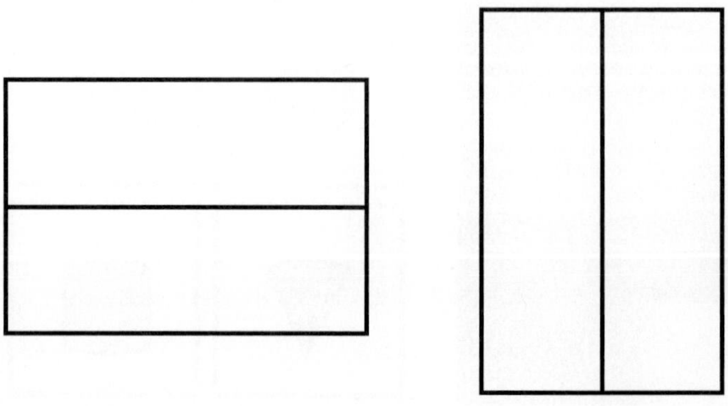

Tree: Ring the cone shape.
Star: Ring the small triangle.
Apple: Ring the shape that shows halves.
Fish: Color one half of each rectangle red.

Chapter 4

Find the Shapes

Talk about the picture. Point out shapes, figures, fair shares, or equal parts.

Home Note: Encourage your child to talk about the shapes in the picture. Then have your child point out shapes in the home.

Draw a ring around one half of the group of
children at each table.

STORY TIME

Listen to the story.
**"The Seeds
Become Flowers"**

Name _____

Dear Family,

   Today we started Chapter 5 in our math book. We will be learning about the numbers 6 through 10 and the positions sixth through tenth. The following activities will help me count and help me learn the names of positions. Thanks for helping me.

                              Love,
                              Your child

Sharing and Doing

Number Match

Help your child make a set of twenty cards. the cards should be numbered 1–10. Each remaining card should have from one to ten pictures on it. Your child can draw the pictures or cut small pictures out of magazines. After the cards are completed, mix them up and see how fast your child can match the picture cards with the number cards.

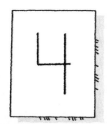 

Variations:
1. Encourage your child to put the picture cards in order from fewest items to most.
2. Encourage your child to put the cards in order and name their positions: first, second, third, and so on.

Use after page 112.

Number Snake

For this activity you will need twelve small paper plates and some crayons and yarn. First, have your child draw a funny face on one plate. Next, have your child write the number 0–10 on the remaining plates. There should be one number per plate. Mix up the plates, and spread them face up on a flat surface.

Have your child select the plates in order, one by one, and place them behind the drawing of the face. When all plates are in order, help your child attach them to one another with yarn. Find a place to display the "number snake." Your child may want to make more number snakes with different designs.

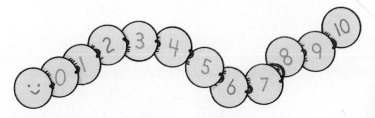

Use after page 106.

6
six

Top: Make a group of five on the branches. Then show one more to make a group of six. Count them. Paste. **Bottom:** Draw six eggs in the nest.

Home Note: Encourage your child to retell the story and make groups of *six* objects.

7 seven

Count the birdhouses. Then draw one more
on the top branch to make a group of seven.
Draw seven birds on the bottom tree branch.

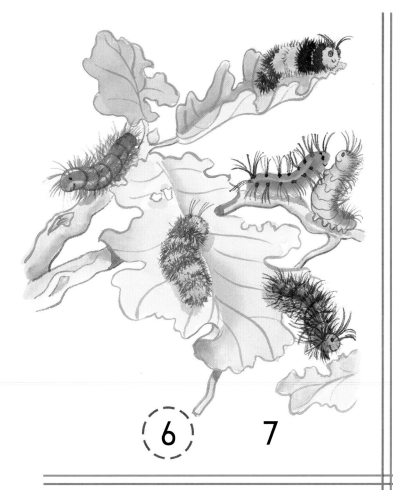

6   7

6   7

6   7

6   7

Put a counter on each object. Count the counters. Ring the correct number.

Home Note: Encourage your child to practice counting groups of *six* and *seven* objects.

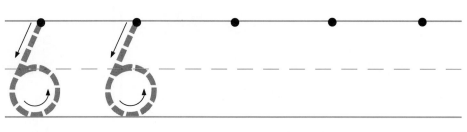

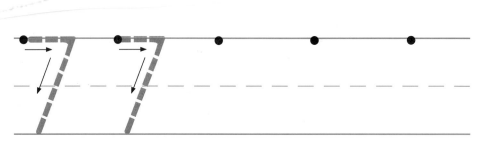

Top: Count. Write the number.
Bottom: Count. Write the number for each.

8 eight

Use punchout acorns to make a group of seven acorns. Then show one more to make a group of eight. Count them. Then remove and draw eight acorns.

Home Note: Encourage your child to retell the story and make groups of *eight* objects.

9 nine

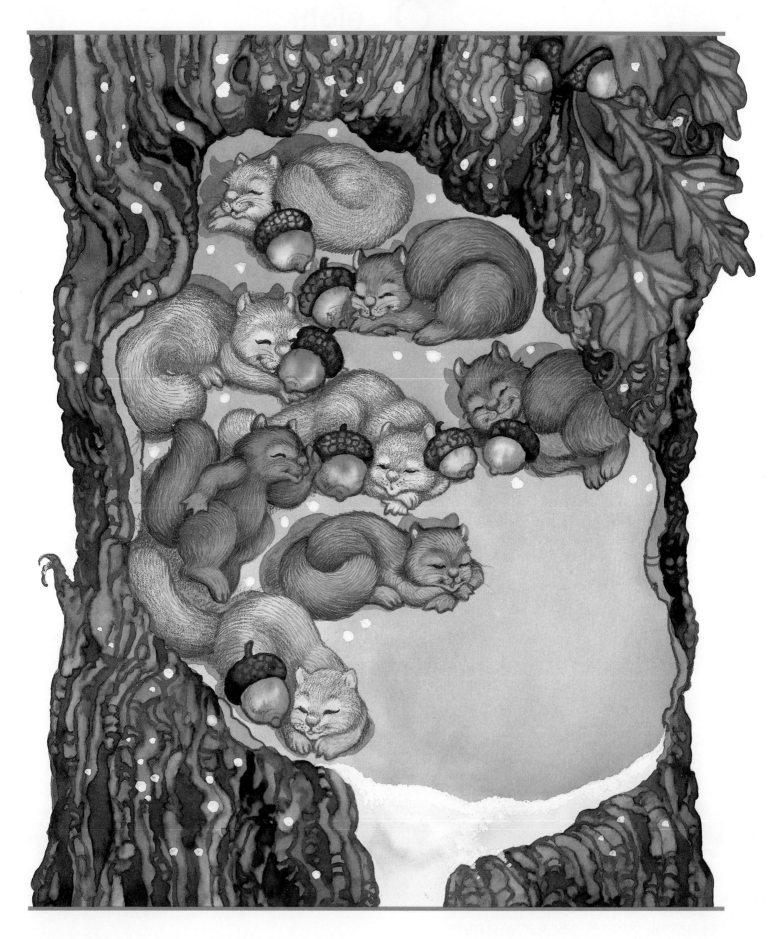

Count the squirrels. Draw more to show nine.

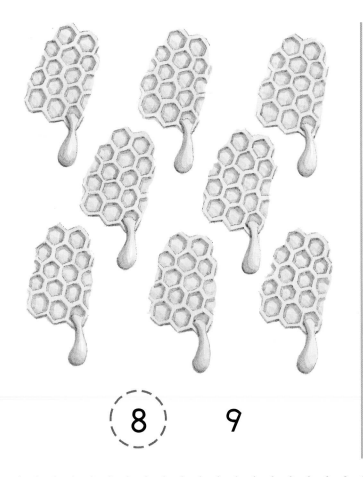

8   9

8   9

8   9

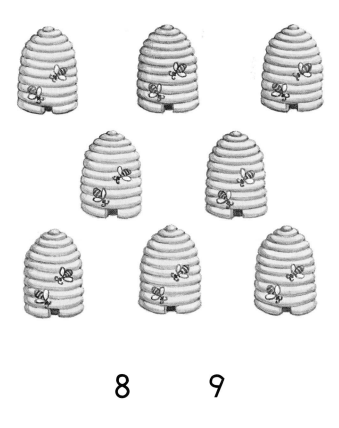

8   9

Put a counter on each object. Count the counters. Ring the correct number.

Home Note: Encourage your child to retell the story and make groups of *eight* and *nine* objects.

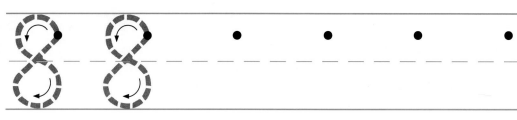

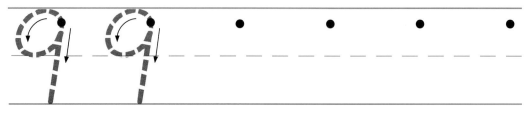

Top: Count. Write the number. **Bottom:** Count how many in the picture. Write the number.

0	1
1	3
2	0
3	2
4	5
5	4
6	8
7	9
8	6
9	7

Draw a line to match each calculator key to the number as it is shown in the window.

Home Note: Encourage your child to become familiar with the number keys on the calculator. Have your child read the numbers in the display window.

Look at your calculator. Put the punchout keys
on the calculator keys where they belong. Paste.

10 **ten**

Top: Make a group of nine. Then show one more to make a group of ten. Count. Then remove the bunnies and draw ten bunny tails in the garden.

Home Note: Encourage your child to retell the story and make groups of *ten*.

103

Ring groups of ten.

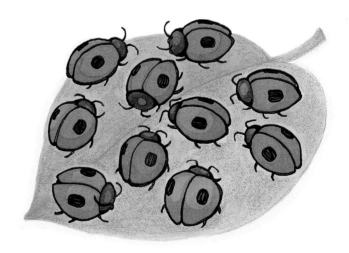

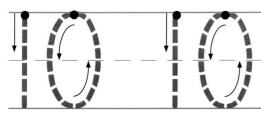

Top: Count. Ring each group of ten. Draw X on each group that does not have ten. **Bottom:** Write the number.

Home Note: Encourage your child to make groups of *ten* objects.

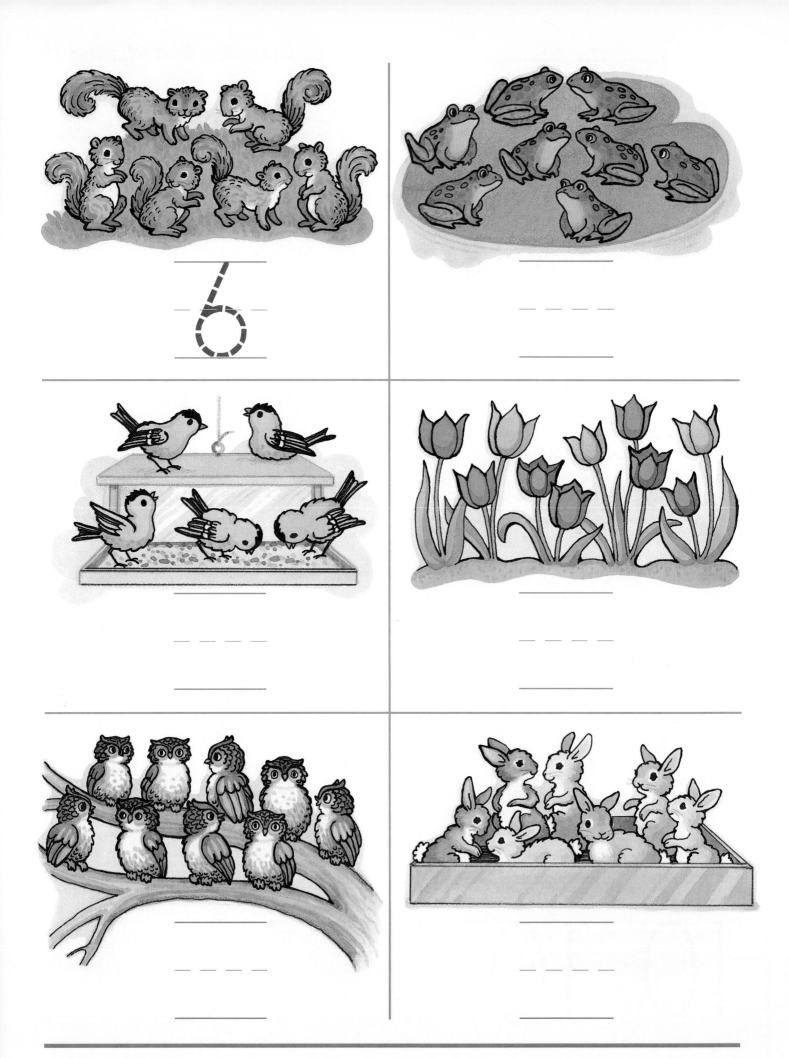

Count the objects in each group. Write how many.

Name _____

Problem Solving

Guess and Check

Guess

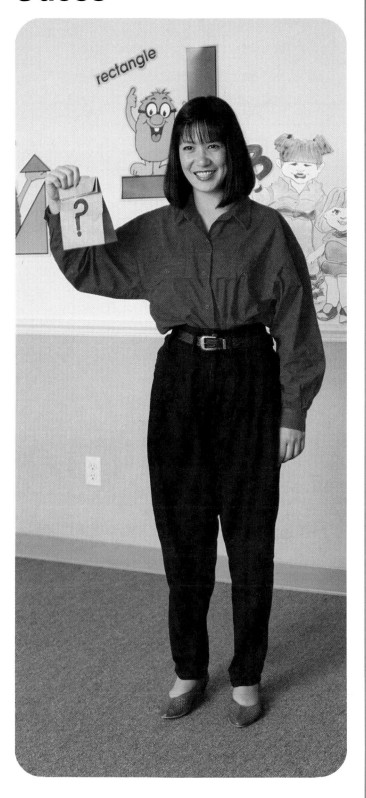

rectangle

More   **Fewer**

Check

Workmat
● ■ ◆

circle

More   **Fewer**

Guess how many counters are in the bag. Are there more or fewer than 5? Ring *More* or *Fewer*. Count the objects. Use the workmat to show how many. Then ring *More* or *Fewer* to show how many were in the bag.

Home Note: Encourage your child to *guess* about how many objects are in a group of ten or fewer objects before counting them. Then have your child count the objects.

107

HBJ material copyrighted under notice appearing earlier in this work.

Number Hunt

0 I 2 3 4 5 6 7 8 9

108 Find the numbers hidden in the picture. Draw X on each number at the bottom as you find it in the picture. Ring the number that is not in the picture.

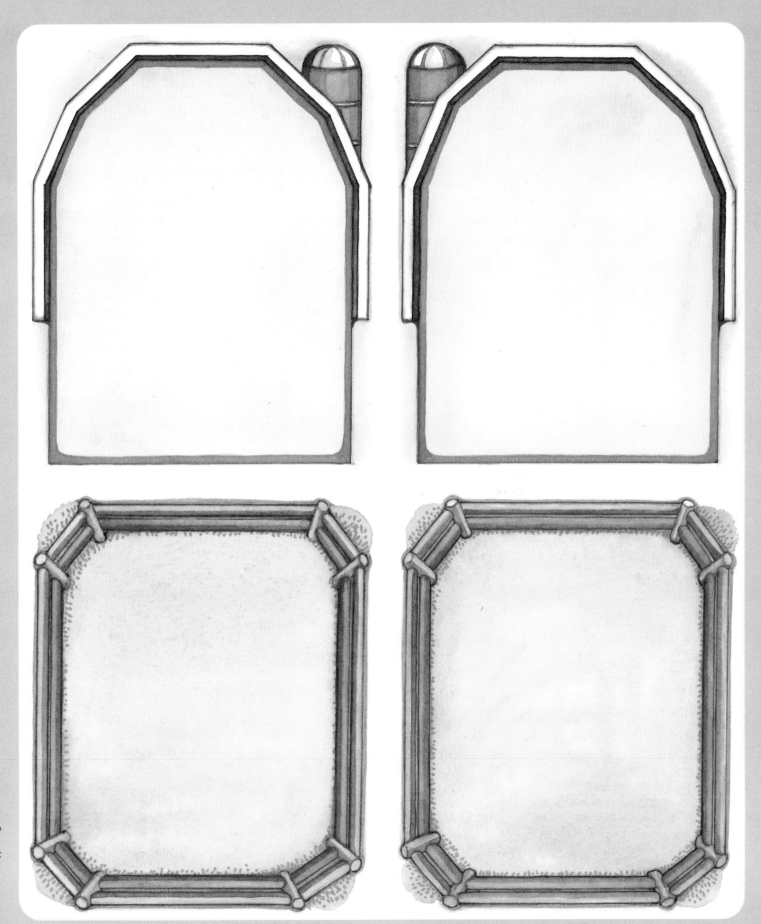

Top: Put some counters in the workspace on the left. Then have your friend count the counters and put the same number of counters in the workspace on the right. Trace and count. **Bottom:** Repeat.

Home Note: Encourage your child to tell you how many counters are in each workspace on the right and why that many counters were drawn.

 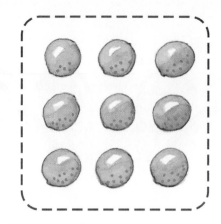 

  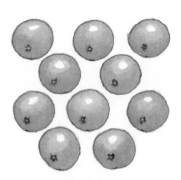

Look at the picture on the left. Count the group of objects. Ring the group on the right that has the same number of objects.

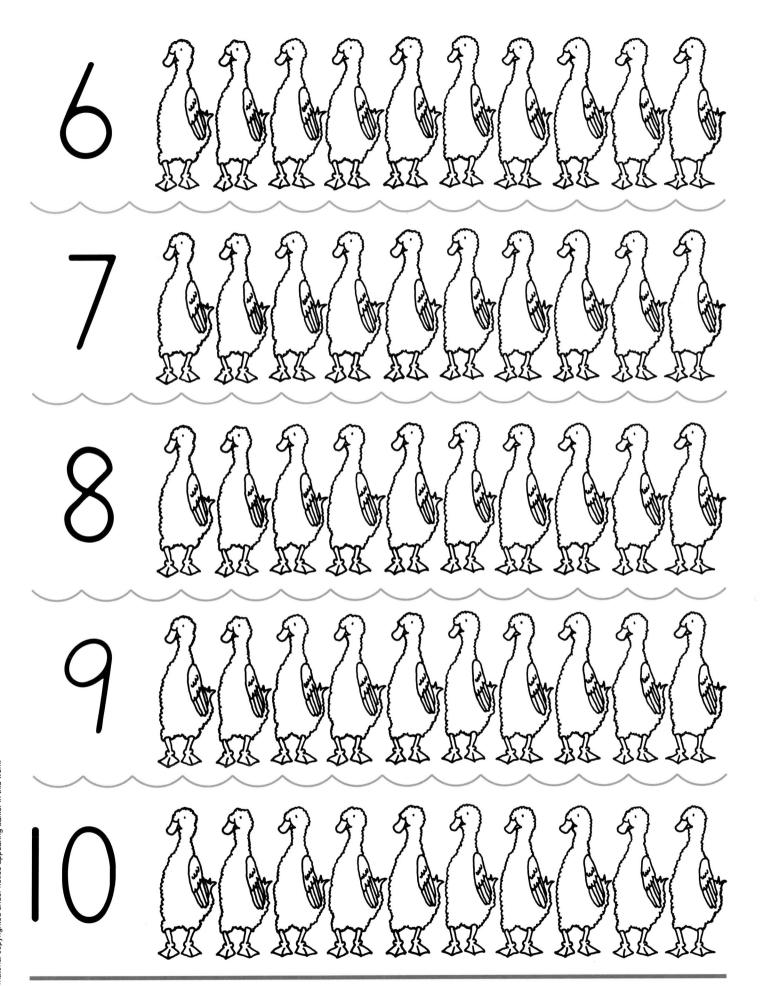

6

7

8

9

10

Color the ducks to show each number.

Home Note: Encourage your child to tell you each number and count the colored ducks in each row.

Write the numbers on the mailboxes in the correct order.

Put counters on frogs to show their positions. Then listen to your teacher and follow the directions.

Home Note: Have your child retell the story using words that tell about each frog's position.

113

Place each frog on a lily pad. Frog with hat is
eighth; flag is sixth; swimsuit is tenth, goggles
are seventh, flippers are ninth.

Count the flowers in the vase on the left. Write
how many flowers. Draw one more than that
many flowers in the vase on the right. Write
how many flowers.

Home Note: Encourage your child to tell
you why that number of flowers was drawn
in each vase.

Count the flowers in the vase on the left.
Write how many flowers. Draw one fewer than
that many flowers in the vase on the right.
Write how many flowers.

Home Note: Have your child explain why
each vase has that number of flowers in it.

Name _____

1	2	3	4	5	6	7	8	9	10

Put a counter on each fish in one group. Color a box for each counter. Do the same for each group.

Home Note: Have your child explain why the boxes are colored as they are.

117

Chapter Review/Test

🌲 _____  _____

⭐

 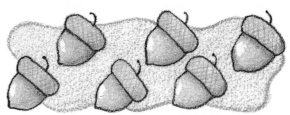

🍎

🐟 7 10 6 9 8

Tree: Count the fish in each group. Write the number. **Star:** Count the objects in each group. Draw a line to match equal groups. Ring the group with one fewer than six. Draw X on the group with one more than six. **Apple:** Draw X on the seventh bird. Ring the ninth bird. **Fish:** Write the numbers in the correct order.

Chapter 5

Talk about the things at camp. Use counters to help you count the objects in each group. Tell which groups have the same number of objects.

Home Note: Encourage your child to point out objects in the picture and count the objects in each group.

How Many More?

🐛	10
🌰	9
🦋	8
🌼	7
🐿️	6

The chart tells how many of each object there should be. Draw more to show that many.

My Little Math Book

by _____

Home Note: Your child may enjoy reading this book to you. You may wish to help your child find and count the animals.

1

_____

_ _ _ _

_____

Find the chipmunks. Ring them. Write the number.

3

_____

- - - -

_____

2   Find the squirrels. Ring them. Write the number.

✂ -

_____

- - - -

_____

4   Find the bunnies. Ring them. Write the number.

Find the carrots. Ring them. Write the number.

5

Ring the seventh duck. Draw X on the ninth duck.

7

Are there more  or  ?

6 Ring the group with more.

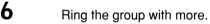

8 Show the same number of baseball mitts as skunks. Draw a baseball mitt for each skunk.

6 Patterns

STORY TIME

Listen to the story.
"A World of Patterns"

School-Home Connection

Dear Family,
    We started a new chapter in our math book today. We will be learning about patterns. Here are some activities for us to do together at home.
                    Love,
                    Your child

Sharing and Doing

What Comes Next?

Gather a collection of two types of objects that differ in size, color, or shape. Some examples might be buttons, beans, or macaroni. Place several objects in a row to make a pattern. Have your child tell you what comes next. Then have your child make a pattern for you to guess what comes next. Chant the pattern together after it is made.

Pattern Hunt

Encourage your child to find patterns at home that repeat. For example, have your child find patterns in wallpaper, table settings, clothing, and furniture. Ask questions such as "Do you see a pattern? What repeats in the pattern? What other patterns can you find?"

Button, bean, bean, button, bean, bean.

Use after page 134.

Use after page 128.

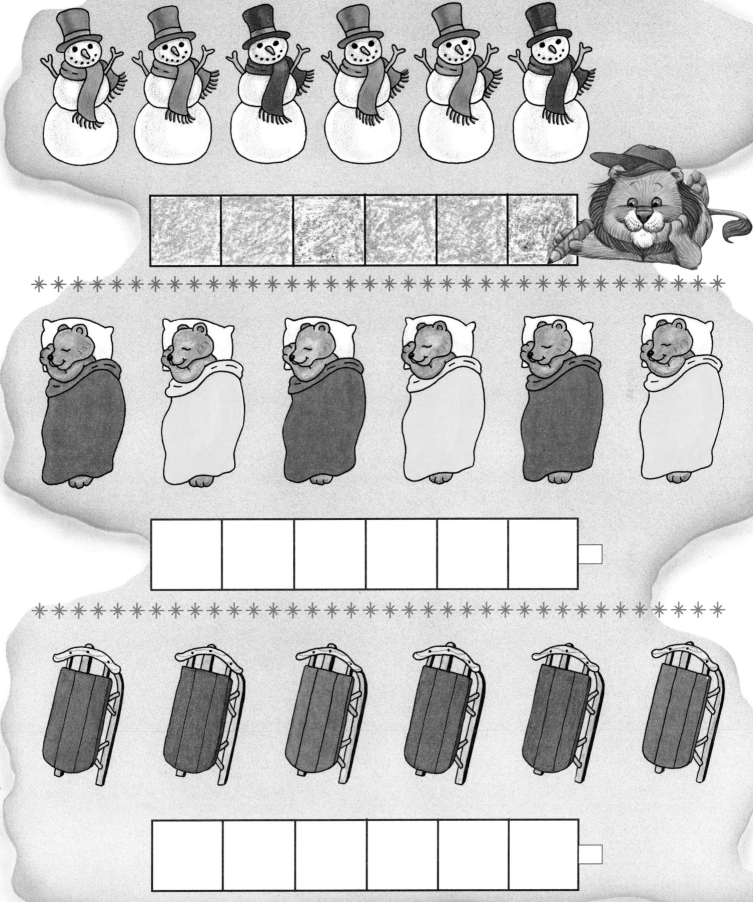

Use connecting cubes to show the pattern.
Color the squares to copy the pattern.

Home Note: Encourage your child to point out each pattern. Talk about other patterns that can be made.

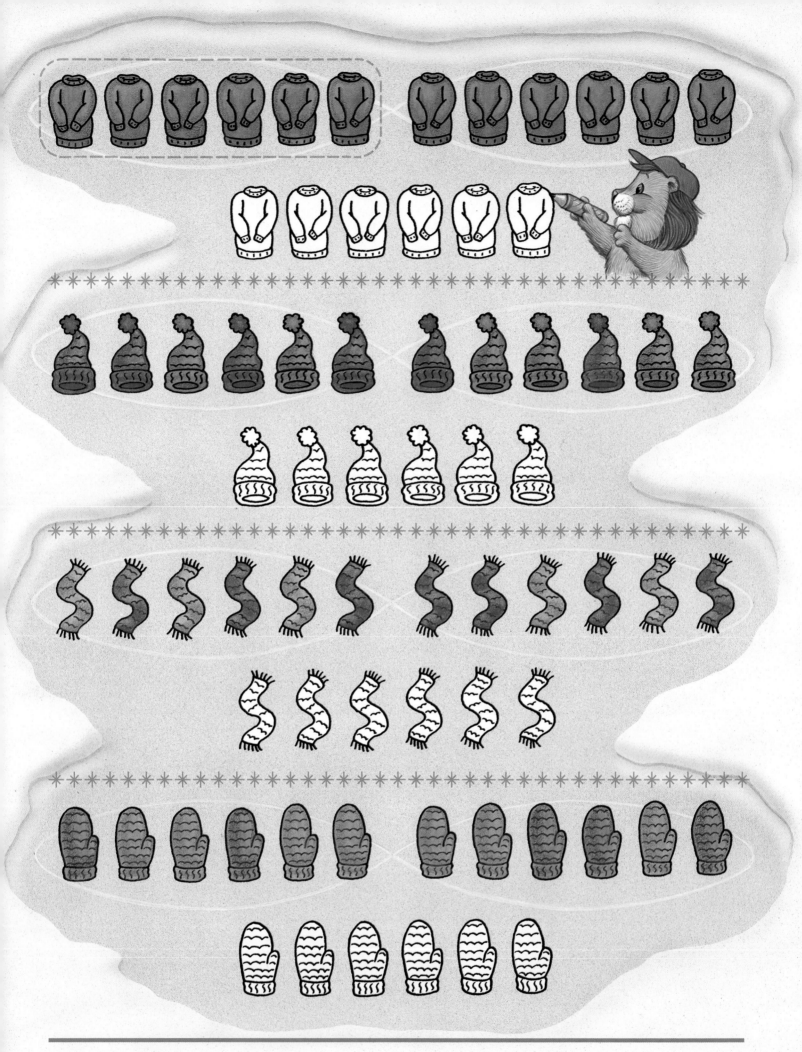

Ring each row that shows a pattern. Color
each bottom row to match the pattern.

Copying Patterns

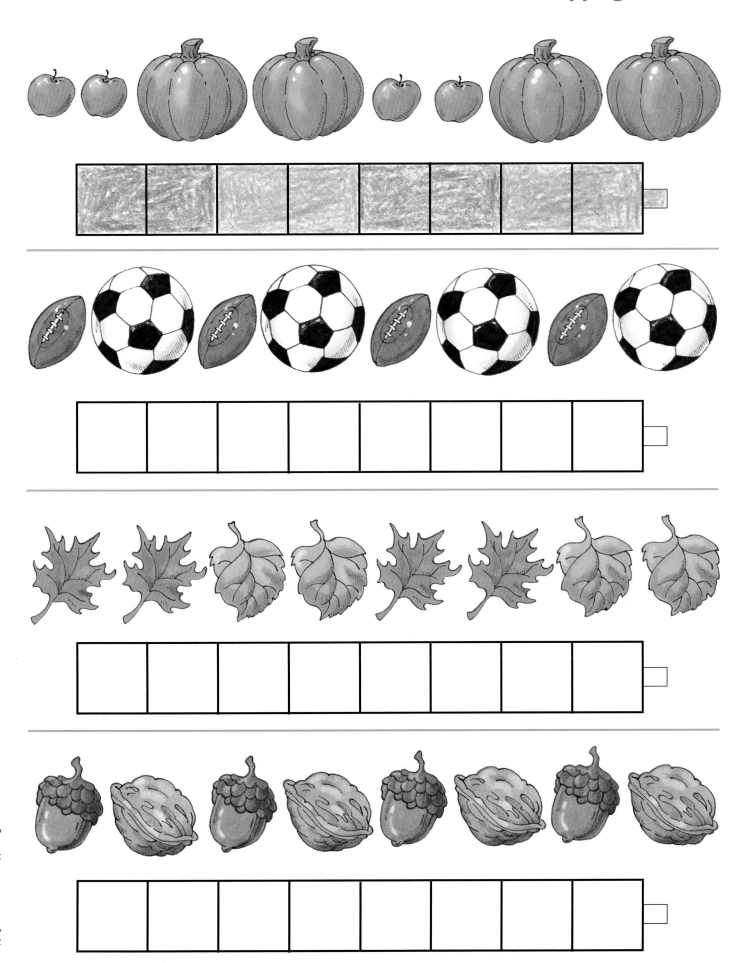

Make a color pattern to match each pattern.

Home Note: Encourage your child to point out each pattern above. Then have your child use objects at home, such as beans or buttons, to copy each pattern.

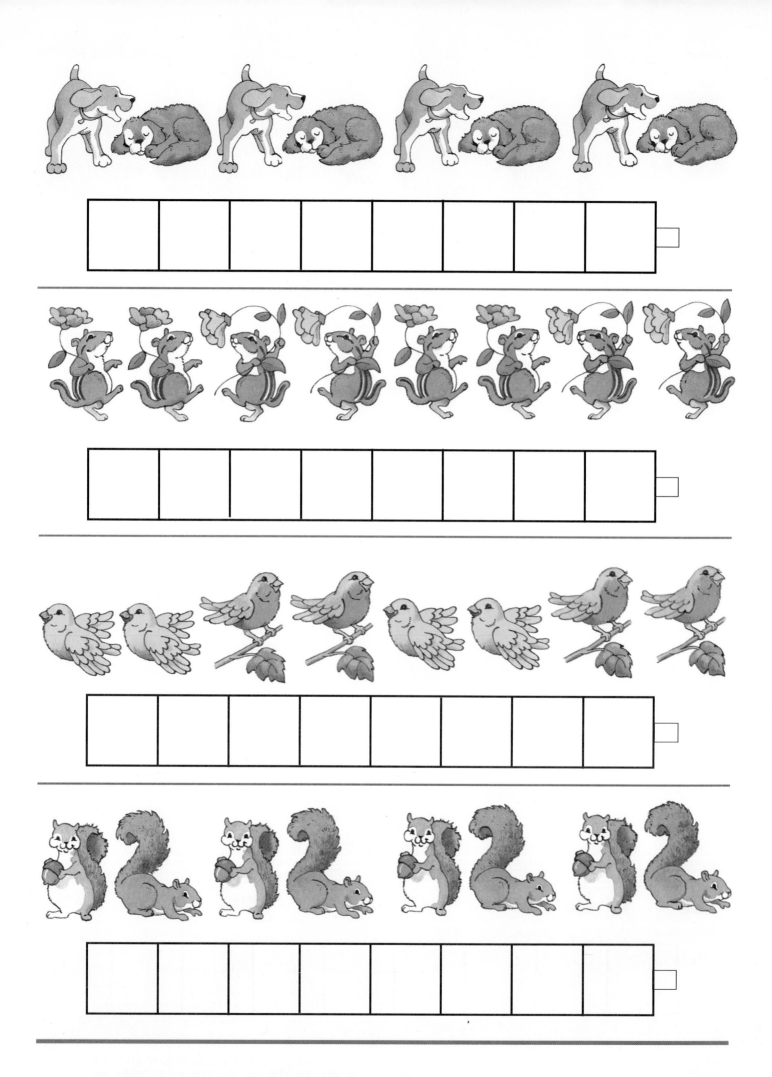

Make a color pattern to match the pattern
made by the animals.

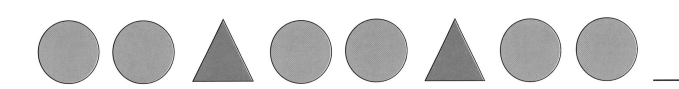

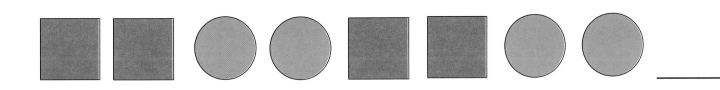

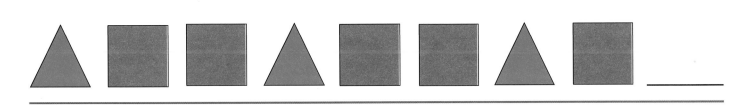

Place pieces on the pattern. Put the shape that comes next. Trace and color it.

Home Note: Encourage your child to point out or "read" each pattern and explain what shape should come next.

127

128   Ring the shape that comes next.

Find a pattern in the stones. Ring the stones that will lead the bear to the den.

Home Note: Have your child explain how the bear found the den.

129

Making a Quilt

Find the pattern in the quilt. Extend the
pattern by coloring the quilt.

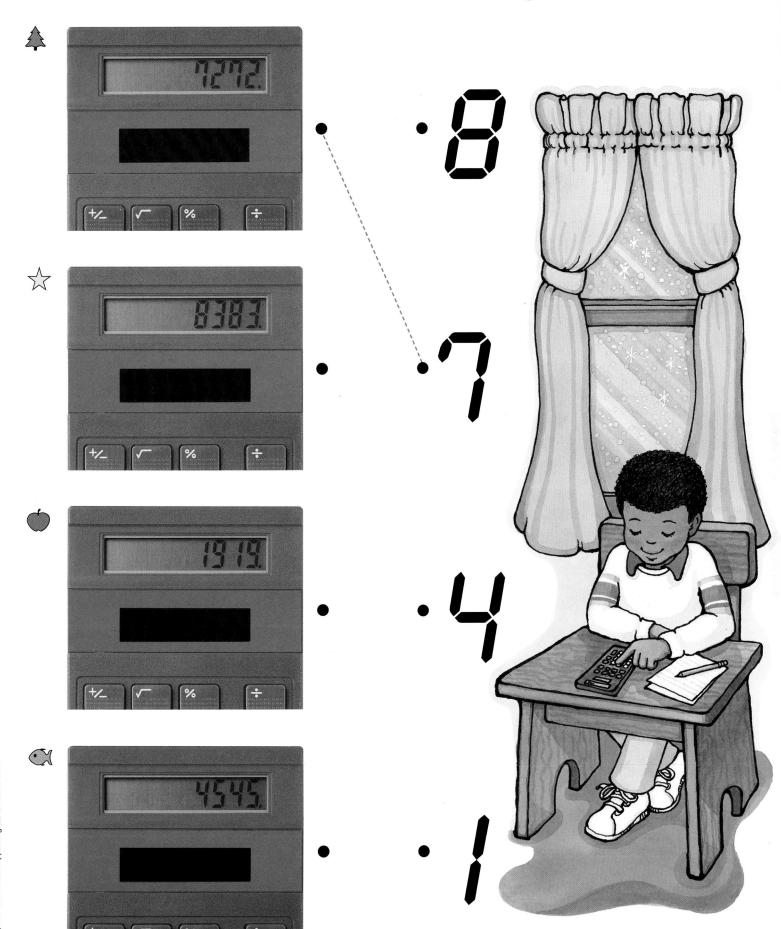

Copy the pattern on a calculator. Then extend the number pattern. Draw a line to the number that comes next.

Home Note: Encourage your child to point out each number pattern. You may wish to have your child create number patterns on a calculator.

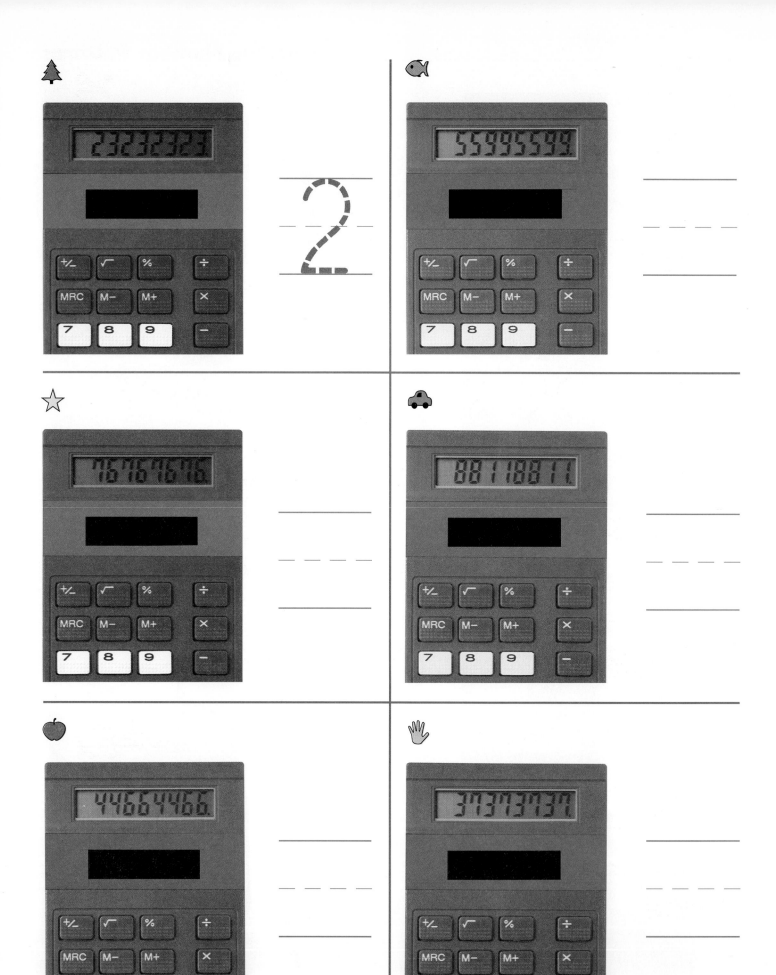

Write the number that comes next.

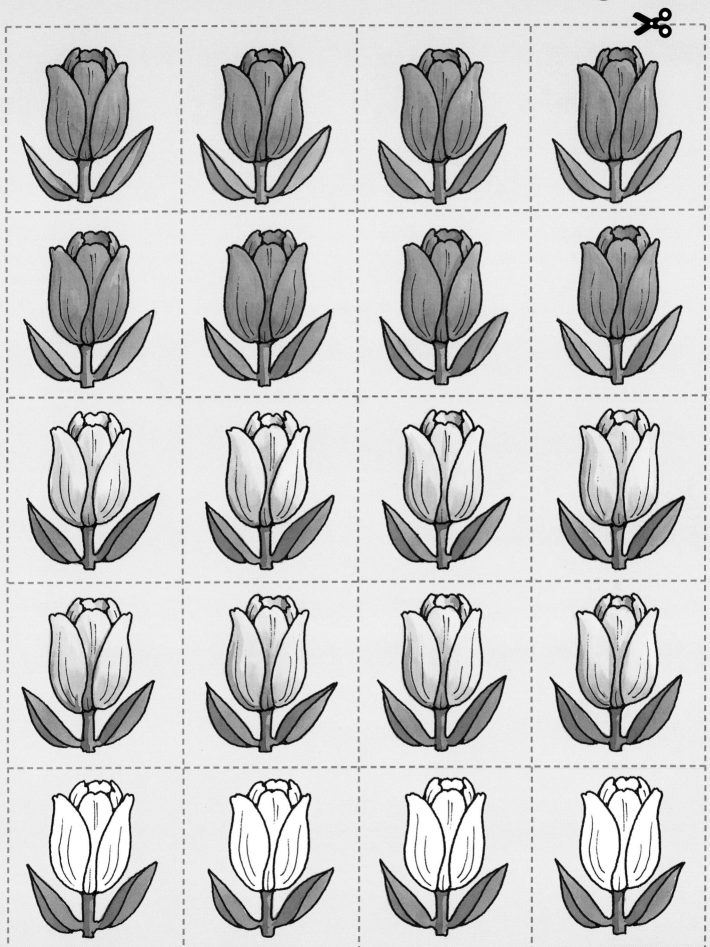

Sort the flowers. Then make a pattern. Color
flowers as needed to complete the pattern.

133

Sort the vegetables. Then make a pattern.
Draw vegetables as needed to complete
the pattern.

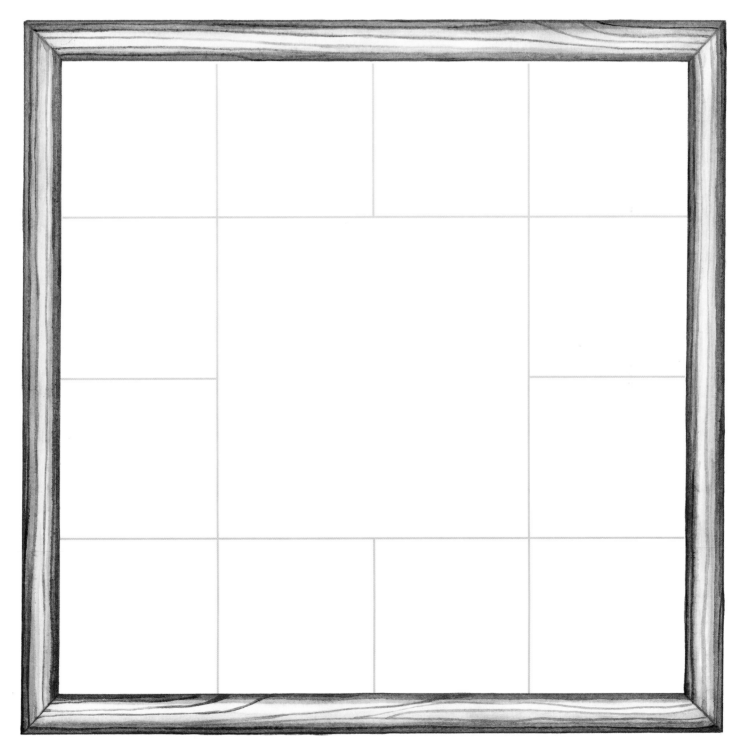

Use cubes to make a pattern. Then color.
Have a friend point out your pattern.
Draw a picture inside the frame.

Home Note: Encourage your child to explain
how the pattern was made.

135

Create a color pattern. Have a friend
point out the pattern.

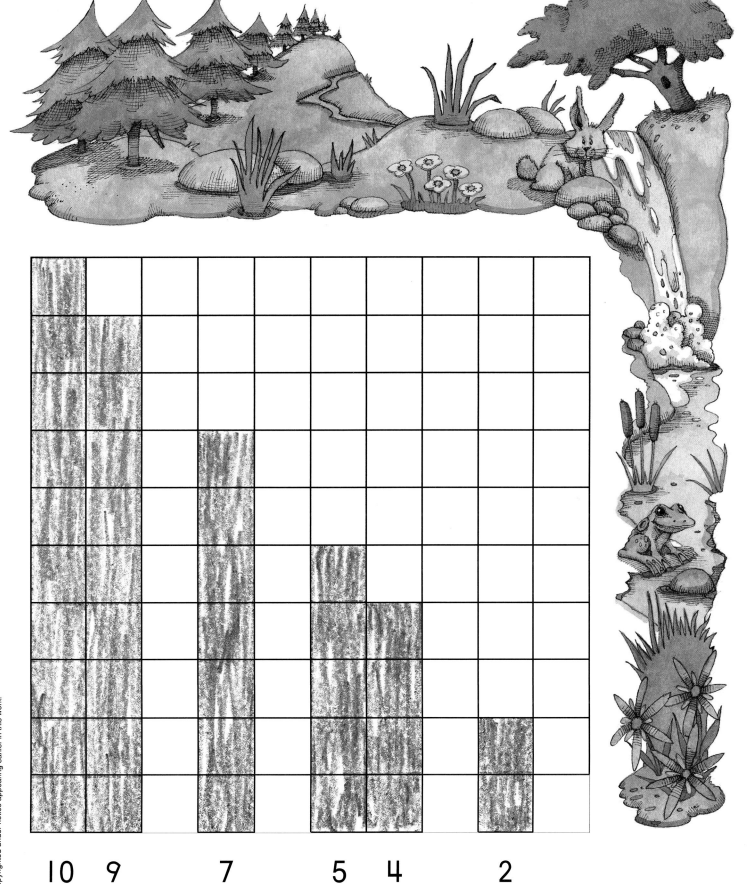

10   9   ____   7   ____   5   4   ____   2   ____

Use connecting cubes to make a model.
Color the boxes. Write the missing numbers.

Home Note: Have your child read the pattern
to you.

137

Chapter Review/Test

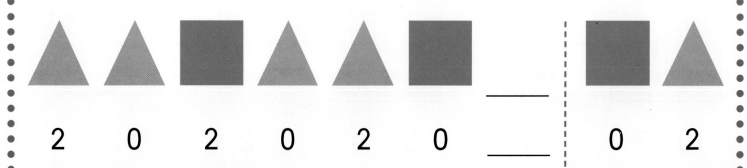

2 0 2 0 2 0 ___ ___ 0 2

Top: Ring the group that shows a pattern.
Choose two crayons and copy the pattern.
Middle: Use crayons to copy the pattern.
Bottom: Ring the one that comes next.

Name _____

Thinking Mathematically
Using a Picture

Talk about the things at the market. Look carefully to find patterns. Ring each pattern.

Home Note: Have your child point out patterns in the picture and read the patterns to you.

139

HBJ material copyrighted under notice appearing earlier in this work.

Find the Missing Pieces

Draw and color the missing piece or pieces in each pattern.

My Little Math Book

by _____

Home Note: Your child may enjoy reading this book to you. You may wish to discuss the seasons with your child and talk about patterns found in the book.

I

✂ -

Home Note: Talk about the patterns.

3

2

4   Color the flowers to show a pattern.

Continue the pattern.

5

 Home Note: Talk about the pattern.

7

6   Color the leaves to show a pattern.

✂ -

8   Color the mittens to show a pattern.

CHAPTER 7

Numbers 11 to 20

STORY TIME

Listen to the story.
"The Cowboy Hat Collection"

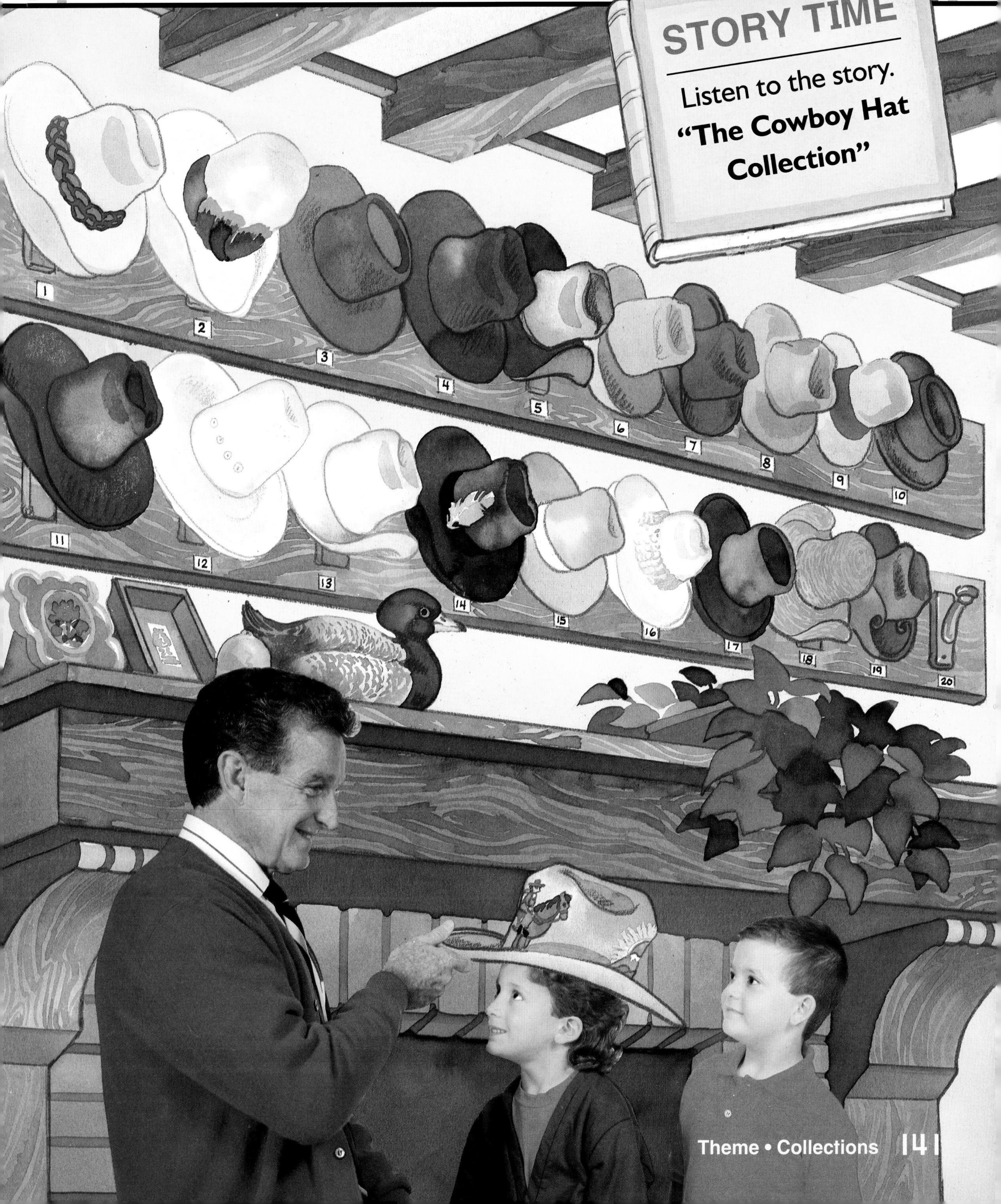
1
2
3
4
5
6
7
8
9
10
11
12
13
14
15
16
17
18
19
20

School-Home Connection

Dear Family,
   We started a new chapter in our math book today. We will be learning about the numbers 11 through 20. Here are some activities for us to do at home together.
                              Love,
                              Your child

Sharing and Doing

What Day Is It?

Have your child make a card for each of the numbers 11 to 20. Each morning have your child pick one card from the set. Discuss the number on the card and declare that day as "Twelve Day" or "Thirteen Day," and so on. Have your child do many things during the day using that number. You may wish to include some of the following:
1. Say hello.
2. Touch his or her toes.
3. Hop or skip.
4. Jump rope.
5. Put that many pennies in a jar.

Use after page 154.

Up on the Rooftop

Help your child make ten houses as shown using colored paper. Draw a set of dots —11 to 20 — on each roof. Ask your child to count the dots on each roof and write the number on the house. When the houses are complete, have your child cut the roofs and houses apart and use them to play a matching game.

Use after page 158.

142

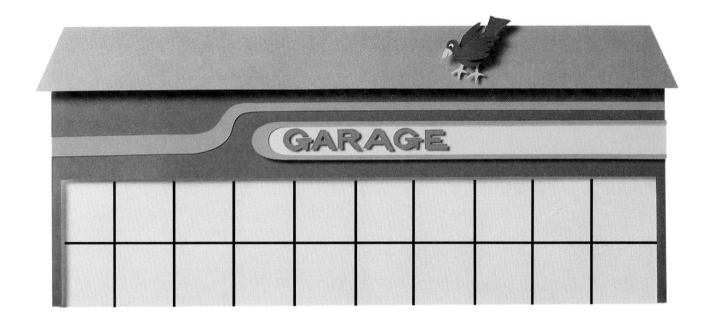

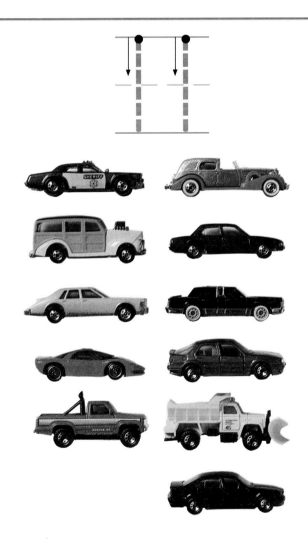

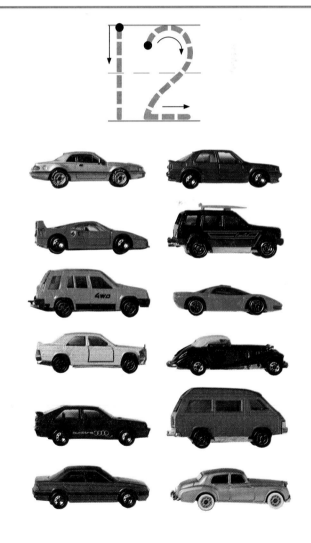

Put a counter on each object. Move the counters to the garage. Count the counters. Trace the number.

Home Note: Encourage your child to count various groups of objects.

143

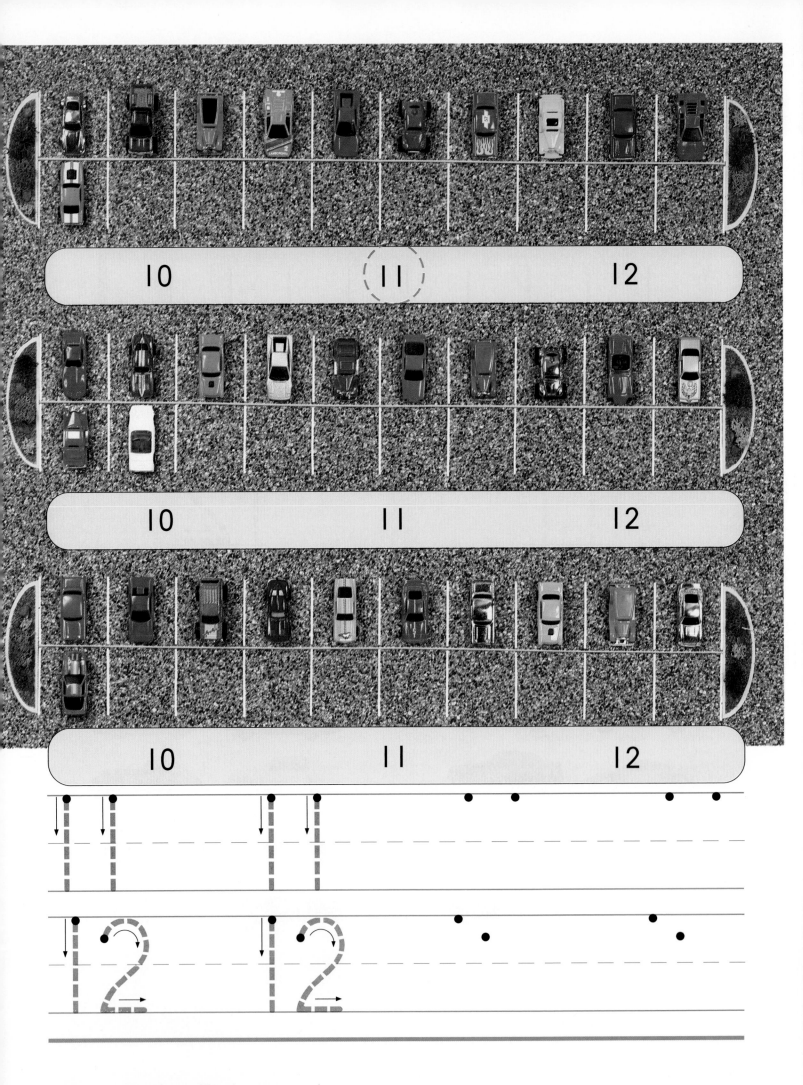

10   (11)   12

10   11   12

10   11   12

Top: Count. Ring the correct number.
Bottom: Write the numbers.

Put a counter on each object. Move the counters to the sticker album. Count the counters. Trace the number.

Home Note: Encourage your child to make groups of 1 less than 14 objects and a group of 1 more than 13.

12   13   14

12   13   14

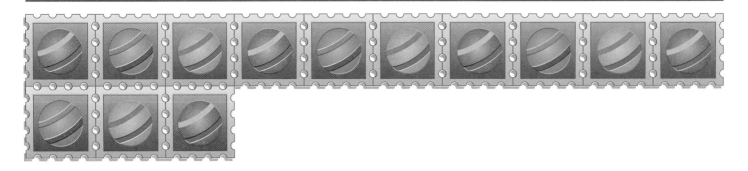

12   13   14

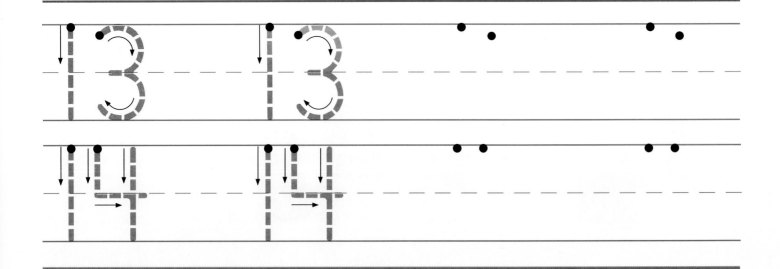

Top: Count. Ring the correct number.
Bottom: Write the numbers.

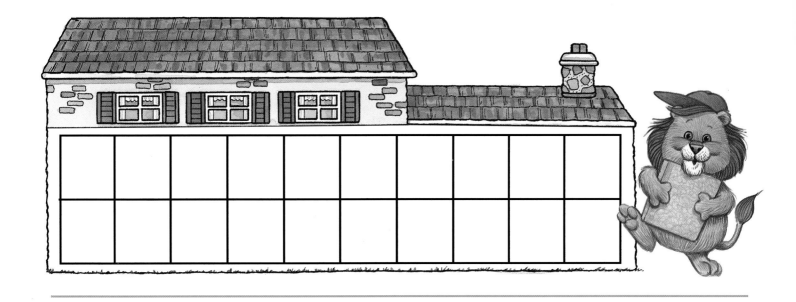

Put a counter on each object. Move the counters to the dollhouse. Count the counters. Trace the number.

Home Note: Encourage your child to make groups of 1 less than 16 objects and 1 more than 15.

147

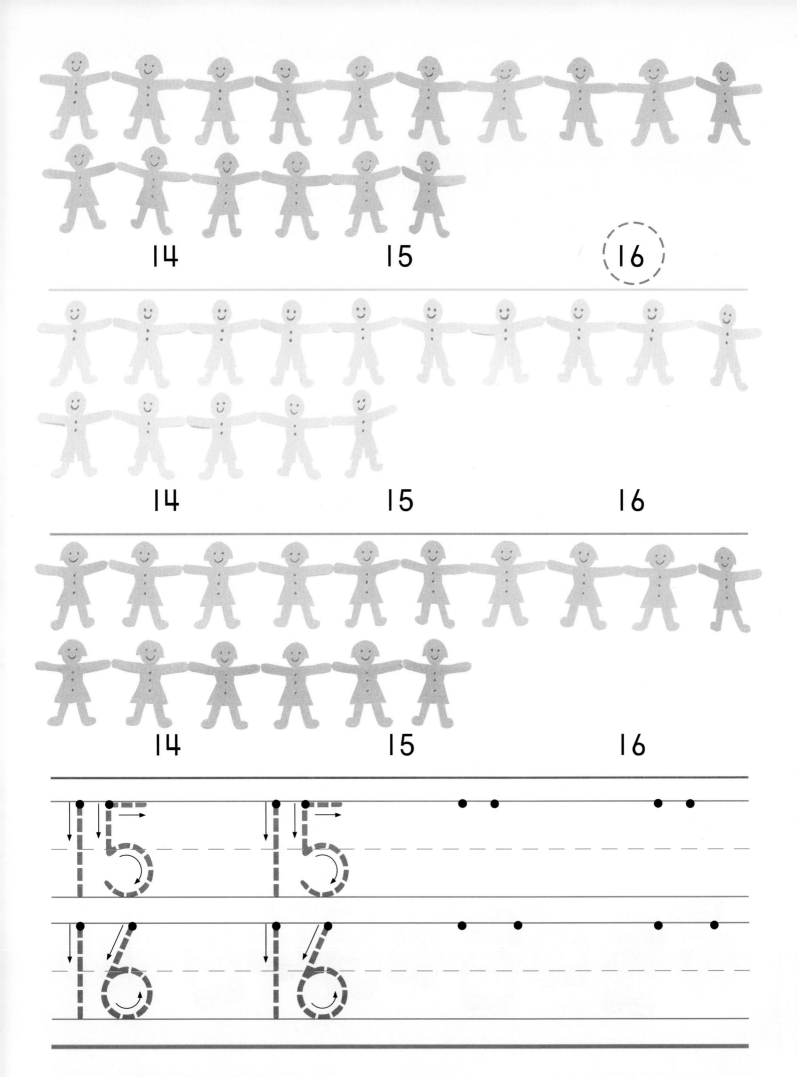

14   15   (16)

14   15   16

14   15   16

148

Top: Count. Ring the correct number.
Bottom: Write the numbers.

O	O	O	O	O	O	O	O	O	O

– – – – – – –

O	O	O	O	O	O	O	O	O	O

– – – – – – –

Guess

o	o	o	o	o	o	o	o	o	o

Check

o	o	o	o	o	o	o	o	o	o

Top: Color a box for each cube that is drawn. Write how many of each color. **Bottom:** Guess how many of each color are in the bag. Color and write how many. Check your guess. Color and write how many.

Home Note: Encourage your child to explain how he or she made the guess.

149

Connect the dots in order.

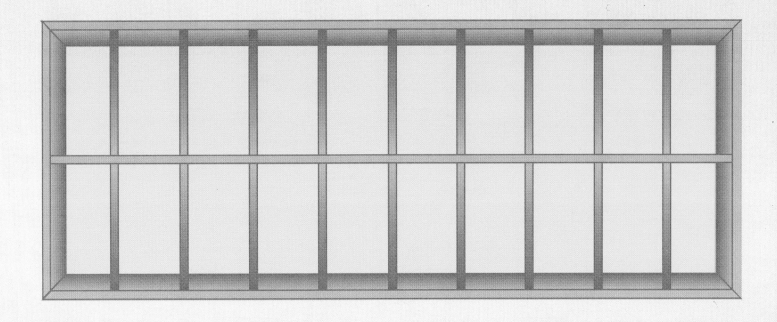

Put a counter on each object. Move the
counters to the box. Count the counters.
Trace the number.

Home Note: Encourage your child to make a
group of 10 and some ones. Have your child
count the objects.

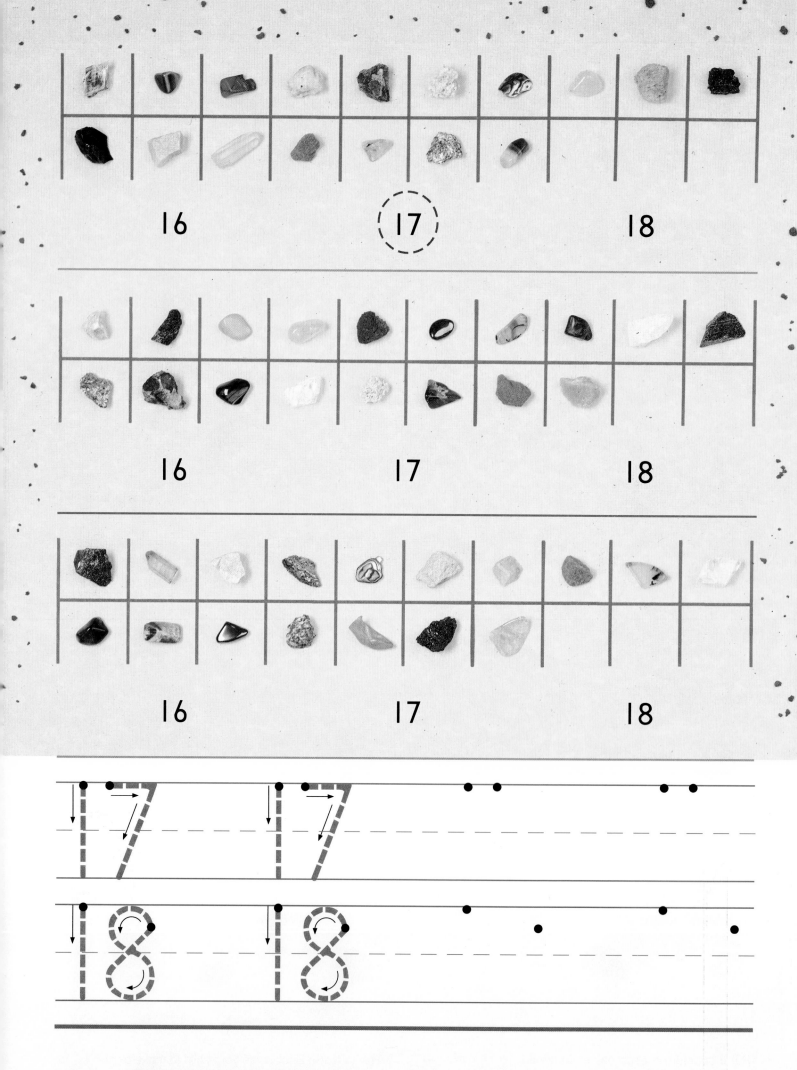

16   (17)   18

16   17   18

16   17   18

7 7

8 8

152

Top: Count. Ring the correct number.
Bottom: Write the numbers.

Name _____ **Counting and Writing 19 and 20**

Put a counter on each object. Move the
counters to the box. Count the counters.
Trace the number.

Home Note: Encourage your child to make
groups of 2 more than 18 and 1 less than 20.

153

18   19   ⟨20⟩

18   19   20

18   19   20

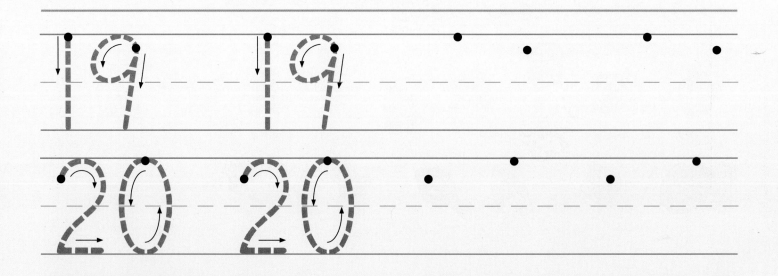

19 19

20 20

154
Top: Count. Ring the correct number.
Bottom: Write the numbers.

11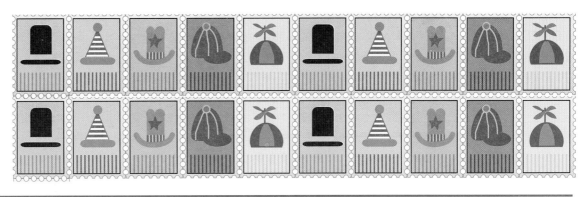

12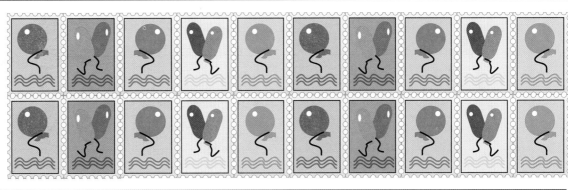

13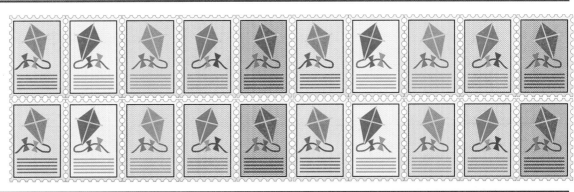

14

15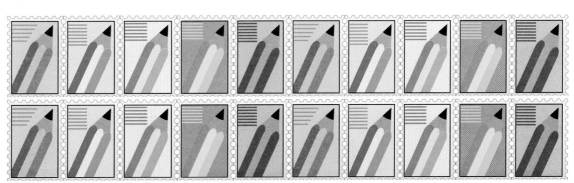

Draw X on the correct number of objects.

Home Note: Encourage your child to make number cards for 11 to 20 and match each card with a group of that many objects.

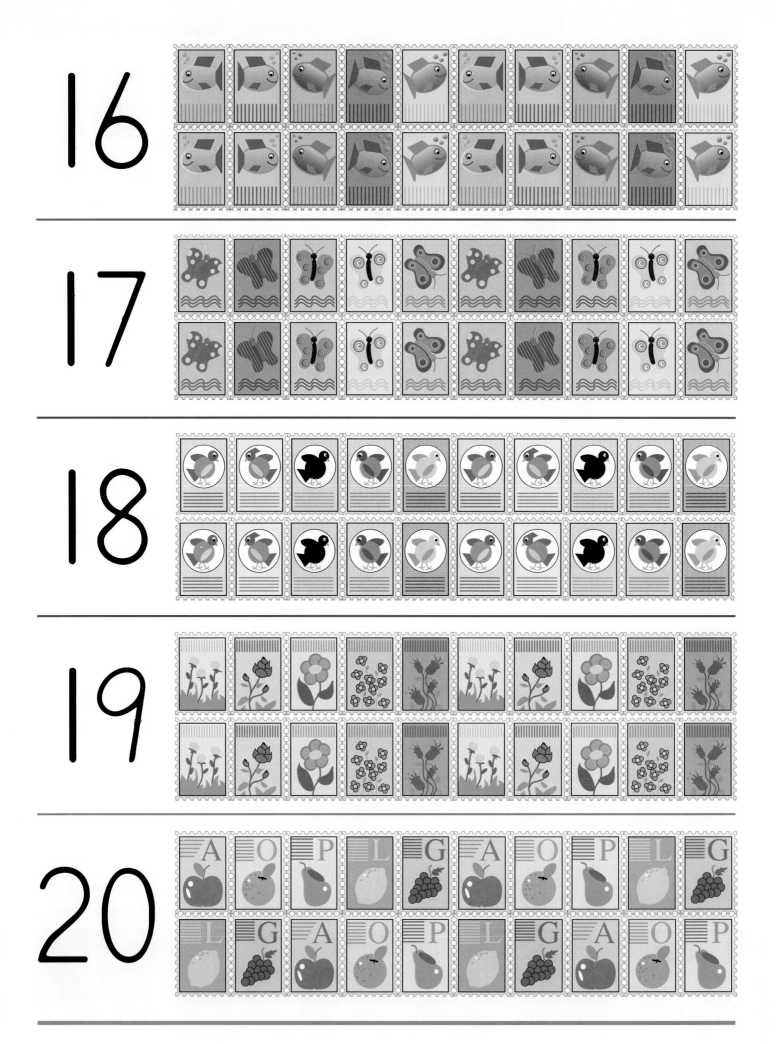

16

17

18

19

20

Draw X on the correct number of objects.

10

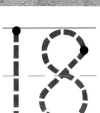

_ _ _ _ _ _ _

_ _ _ _ _ _ _

_ _ _ _ _ _ _   _ _ _ _ _ _ _

_ _ _ _ _ _ _   _ _ _ _ _ _ _

_ _ _ _ _ _ _   _ _ _ _ _ _ _

_ _ _ _ _ _ _   _ _ _ _ _ _ _

_ _ _ _ _ _ _   _ _ _ _ _ _ _

Guess how many. Write your guess. Count
the shells. Write how many.

Home Note: Encourage your child to
estimate how many before counting
groups of objects.

Chapter Review/Test

| 11 | 12 | 13 | 14 | 15 | 16 | 17 | 18 | 19 | 20 |

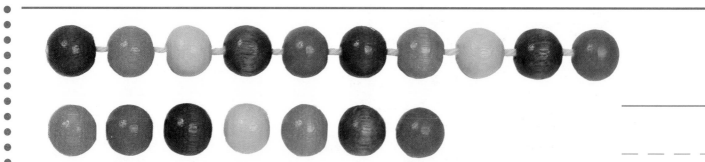

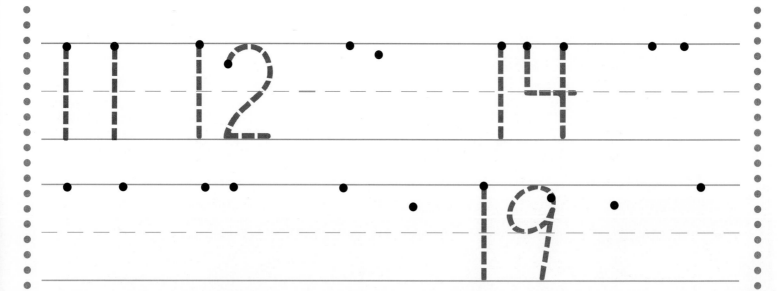

11 12   14

9

Top and middle: Count the objects. Write the number. **Bottom:** Write the numbers in order.

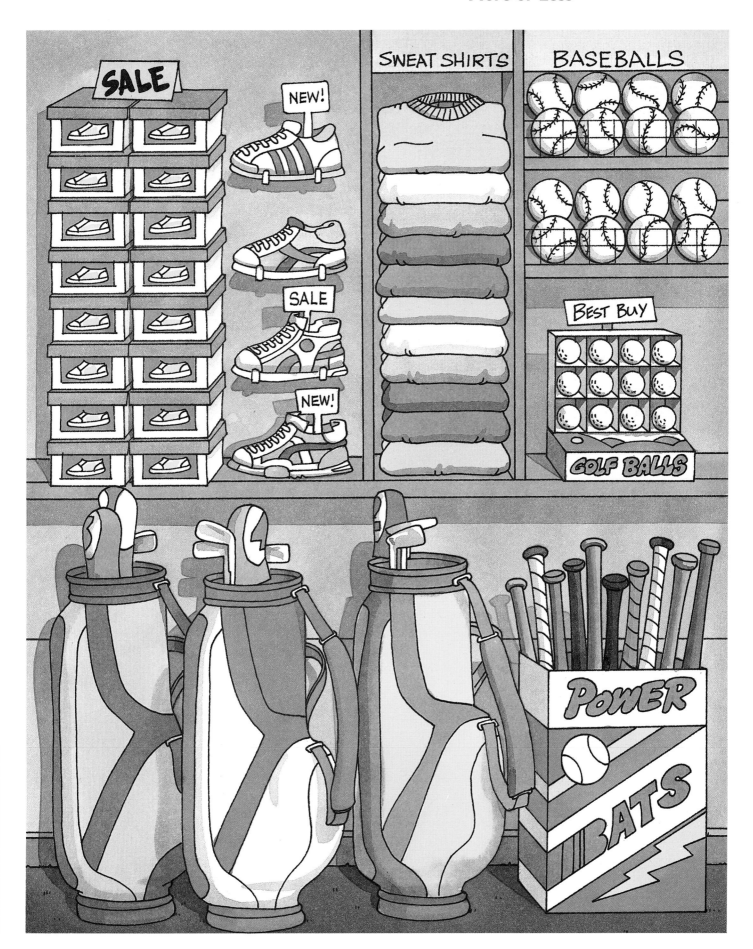

Talk about the picture. Count the groups of objects. Ring the groups that have more than 15 objects.

Home Note: Encourage your child to count groups of objects. Have your child tell which groups have less than 15 objects.

Parts of the Computer

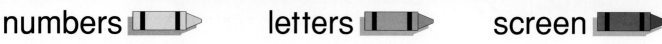

numbers ▭▶   letters ▭▶   screen ▭▶

→ ↑ ▭▶   (RETURN) ▭▶   spacebar ▭▶

Find and color the parts of the computer.

My Little Math Book

by _____

 Home Note: Your child may enjoy reading this book to you. You may wish to have your child count as he or she reads each page.

I

- - - - - - - - - - ✄

_____

__ __ __ __

_____

Count the shells. Write how many.   **3**

_____

- - - - -

_____

2   Count the shells. Write how many.

_____

- - - - -

_____

4   Count how many. Write the number.

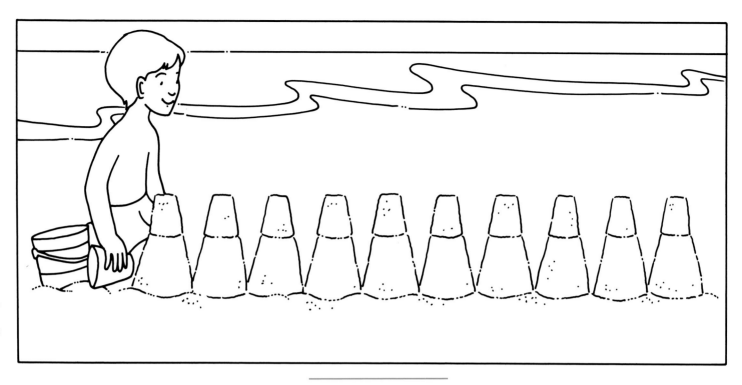

Count how many. Write the number.

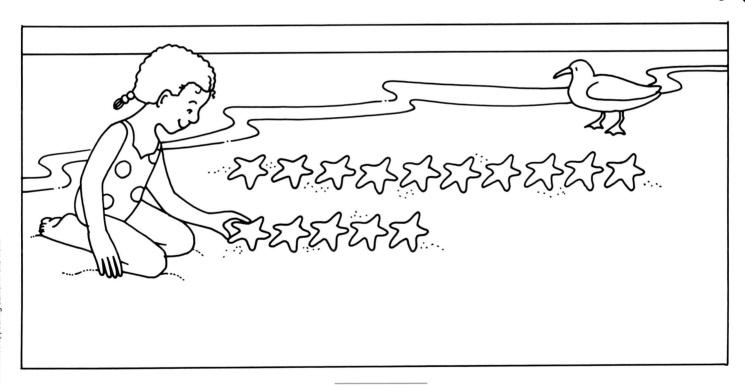

Draw 3 more starfish. Then count how many.
Write the number.

──────────

─ ─ ─ ─

──────────

6   Count the starfish. Write how many.

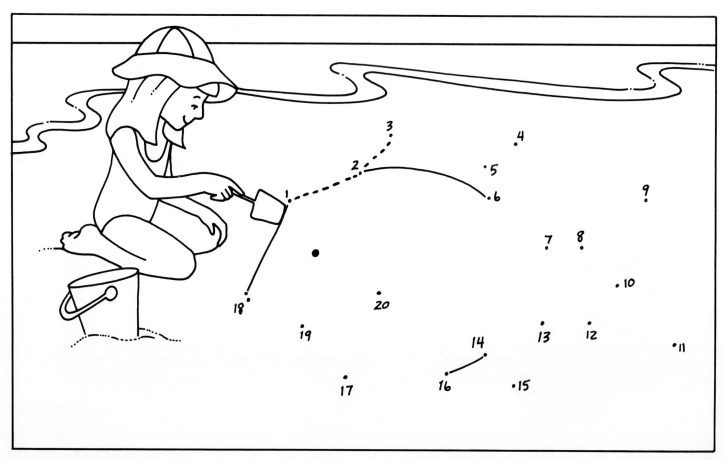

8   Count to 20. Connect the dots as you count.

STORY TIME

Listen to the story.
"The Bike-a-Thon"

School-Home Connection

Dear Family,
  We started a new chapter in our math book today. We will be learning about time and money. Here are some activities for us to do together at home. These activities will help me learn about telling time and counting money.
                    Love,
                    Your child

Sharing and Doing

What Time Is It?

Talk with your child about things he or she does at specific times of the day. For example, what time does your child

• get up?
• eat breakfast?
• go to school?
• get home from school?
• eat dinner?
• go to bed?

Then talk with your child about how long it takes to empty the trash, rake the yard, eat a meal, and so on.

Use after page 172.

What Can I Buy Today?

Place ten pennies, two nickels, and one dime in an envelope, an old purse, or a wallet. Have your child help you make ten price tags as follows: 1¢, 2¢, 3¢, 4¢, 5¢, 6¢, 7¢, 8¢, 9¢, 10¢. Each day, place one of the price tags on a toy or other object in your home. Give your child the envelope of money, and have him or her "buy" the toy using only one kind of coin.

Use after page 180.

2   1   3

Number to show what happened first,
next, and last.

Home Note: Encourage your child to
retell the stories using the words ***first***,
next, and ***last***.

165

3   1   2

___   ___   ___

- - -   - - -   - - -

___   ___   ___

- - -   - - -   - - -

166 Number to show what happened first, next, and last.

Ring the activity that takes more time.

Home Note: Encourage your child to tell you which activities might take *more time* or *less time* than others.

Ring the activity that takes less time.

Name _____

Guess

Check

Guess which takes more time. Ring it. Check your guess. Ring what took more time.

Home Note: Name a simple task. Encourage your child to guess whether the task can be done in *one minute*. Then have your child complete the task and tell how long it took.

169

Ring the activities that can be done in one
minute or less.

8 o'clock

Write the numbers on the clock. Color the hour hand red and the minute hand blue.

Home Note: Encourage your child to point out the parts of the clock.

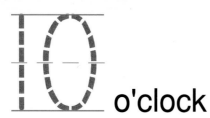 o'clock

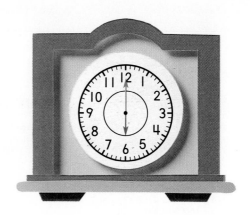

_____ o'clock

_____ o'clock

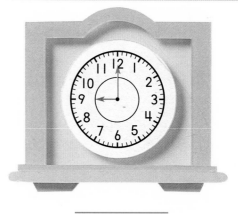

_____ o'clock

_____ o'clock

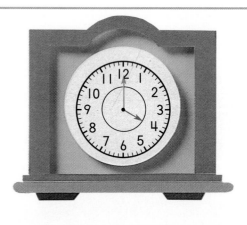

_____ o'clock

Write the number that tells the hour.

9:00   10:00

4:00   5:00

1:00   2:00

7:00   8:00

5:00   6:00

3:00   4:00

Ring the digital clock that shows the same hour as the standard clock.

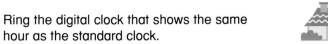

Home Note: Encourage your child to become familiar with digital clocks and reading time on the hour.

Write the time on the digital clock to match.

penny

 or      **nickel**

 or

2 pennies   _____ pennies

_____ nickels   _____ nickels

Top: Put your pennies on the pennies and count. Write how many. **Bottom:** Put your nickels on the nickels and count. Write how many.

Home Note: Encourage your child to point out the *pennies* and *nickels* in each bank. You may wish to have your child identify real coins.

175

penny

 or

nickel

 or

Ring the pennies. Draw X on the nickels.

penny

 or

1¢   1¢

nickel

 or

5¢   5¢

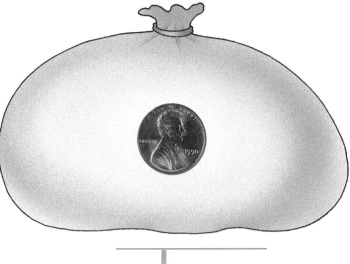

____ ¢

____ ¢

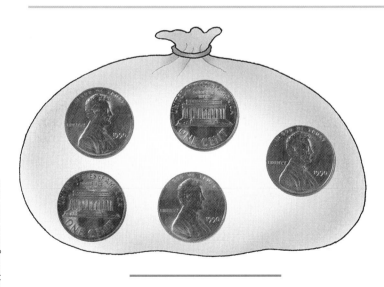

____ ¢

____ ¢

Count the money in each bag and write how much under the bag. Match the coins with a coin of the same value and paste in the box. Write the value of the coin under the box.

Home Note: Encourage your child to make groups of five pennies and trade each group for a nickel.

penny

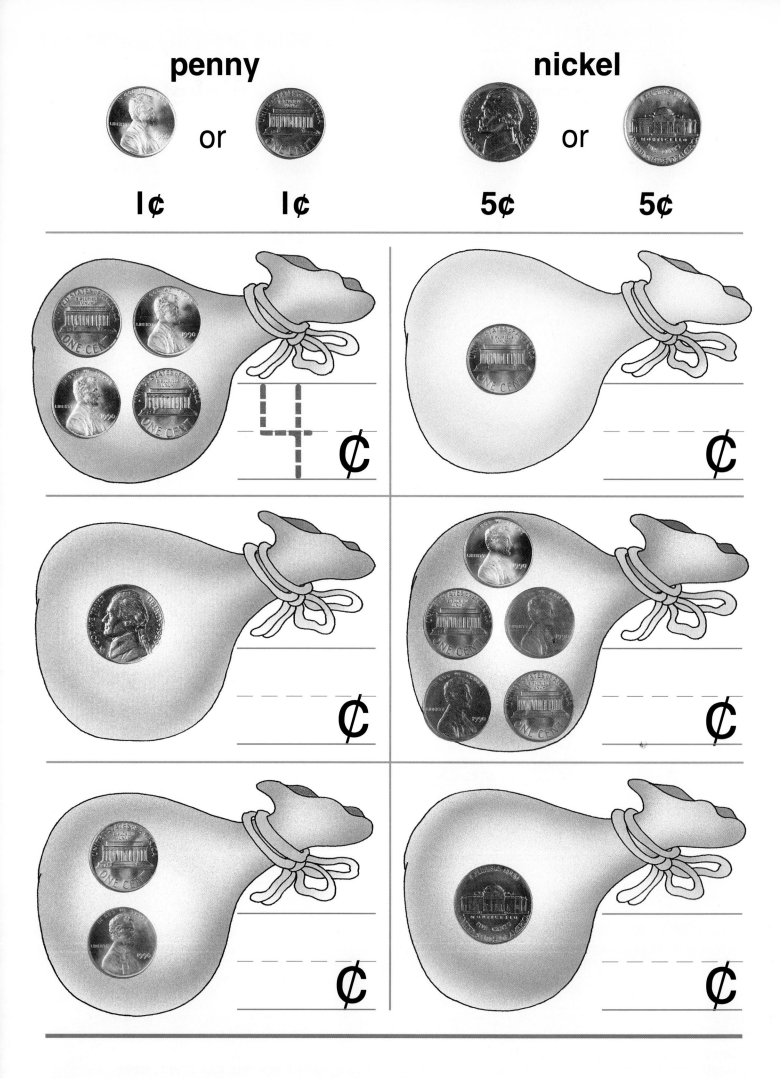

or

1¢   1¢

nickel

or

5¢   5¢

4 ¢

___ ¢

___ ¢

___ ¢

___ ¢

___ ¢

Count the money in each bag. Write how much.

Play store by using coins to buy the objects.

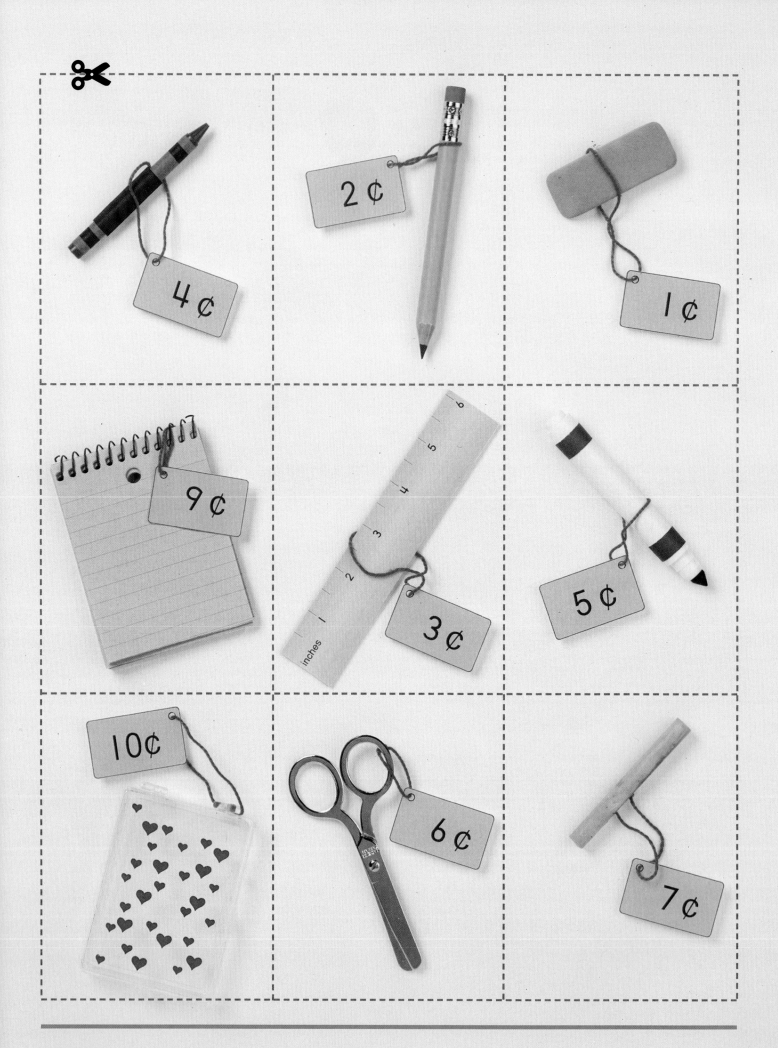

Play store by using coins to buy the objects.

dime

 or

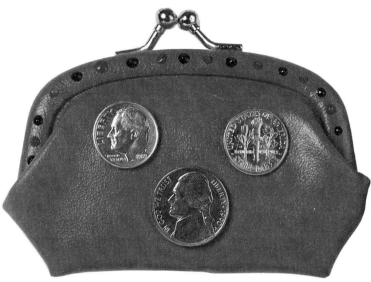

2 ____ dimes

_____ dimes

_____ dimes

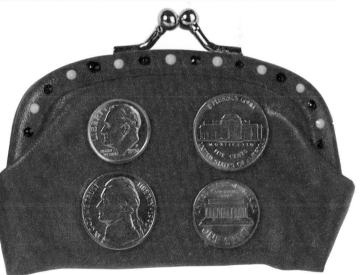

_____ dime

Put your dimes on the dimes. Count.
Write how many dimes.

Home Note: Encourage your child to sort a
collection of *pennies*, *nickels*, and *dimes* and
identify each group.

penny

 or

1¢   1¢

dime

 or

10¢   10¢

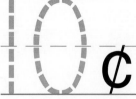 ¢

_____ ¢

Count the money in the blue purse. Write how much. In the green purse, paste the coin that can be traded for the money in the blue purse. Write how much.

182

Choose coins needed to buy each toy.
Paste the coins next to the toy.

Home Note: Encourage your child to trade
pennies for nickels and dimes.

183

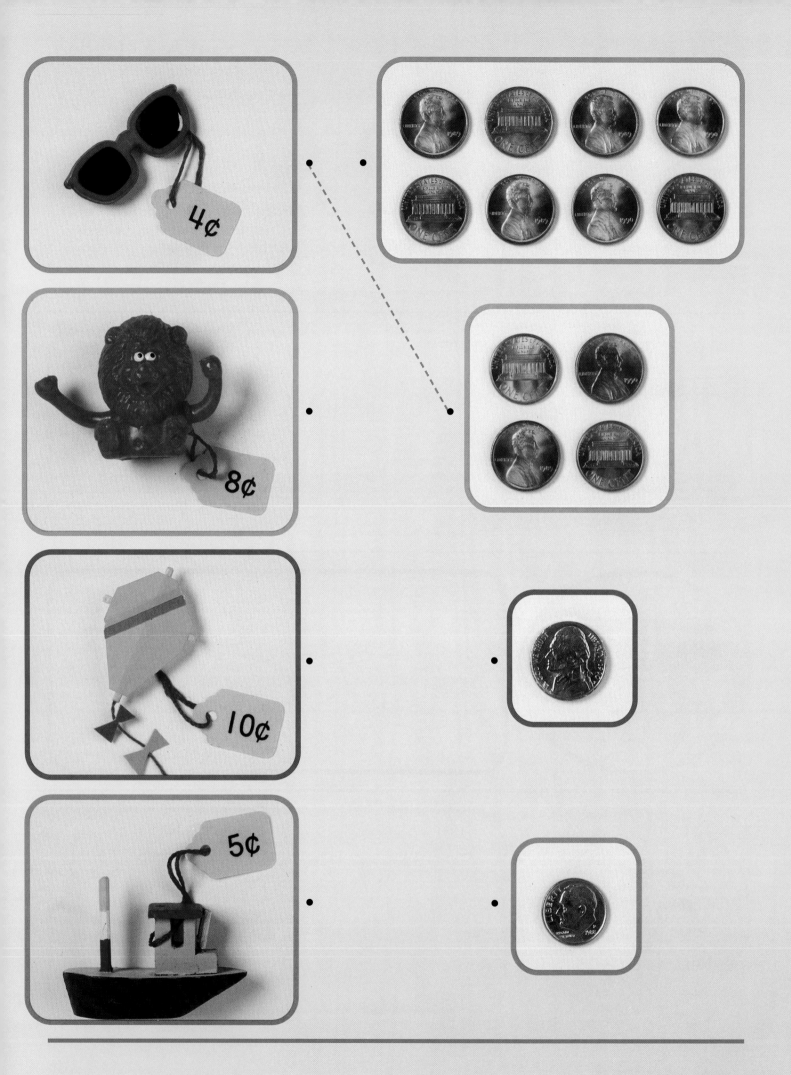

Draw lines to match.

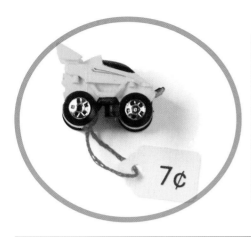

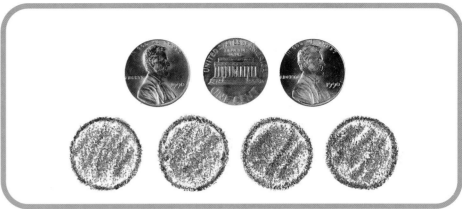

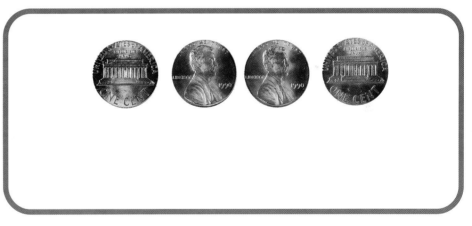

How much more money do you need? Use pennies to act it out. Then draw the pennies you need. Count all the money to check.

Home Note: Mark prices on items and encourage your child to play "store" by counting pennies to purchase each item.

185

Top: Match the hours. Draw lines between clocks.
Middle: Draw lines to match. **Bottom:** Write 1, 2,
and 3 to show what happened first, next, and last.

Name _____

Who Finished First?

Listen to the story. Use punch-outs to
show who finished first, next, and last.

187

Toy Store

5 ¢   6 ¢   7 ¢   ⬤ 7 ¢

5 ¢   ___ ¢   ___ ¢   ___ ¢   ___ ¢

10 ¢   11 ¢   ___ ¢   ⬤ ___ ¢

___ ¢   ___ ¢   ___ ¢   ___ ¢   ⬤ ___ ¢

Write the amount as each coin is counted.
Then write how much each toy costs.

My Little Math Book

by _____

HBJ material copyrighted under notice appearing earlier in this work.

Home Note: Your child may enjoy reading this book to you. Encourage your child to talk about things he or she does at different times of the day.

1

HBJ material copyrighted under notice appearing earlier in this work.

3

2

Ц

5

7

6

_____   _____   _____

_____   _____   _____

_____   _____   _____

Write the numbers 1, 2, and 3 to show what
Donna did first, next, and last.

STORY TIME

Listen to the story.
"Decorating the Classroom"

School-Home Connection

Dear Family,
    We started a new chapter in our math book today. We will be learning about measurement. Here are some activities for us to do together at home.
              Love,
              Your child

Sharing and Doing

Which Jar Holds More?

Show your child a large jar and a small jar. Ask your child which one he or she thinks will hold more water. Help your child fill the small jar and empty it into the large one. Did your child guess right? Continue this activity with jars that are closer to the same size.

Use after page 202.

As Long As My Arm

Help your child cut a string that is the same length as your child's arm. Encourage your child to use this string to find out which things in the house are longer or shorter than his or her arm. You may wish to make lists or have your child draw pictures.

Use after page 196.

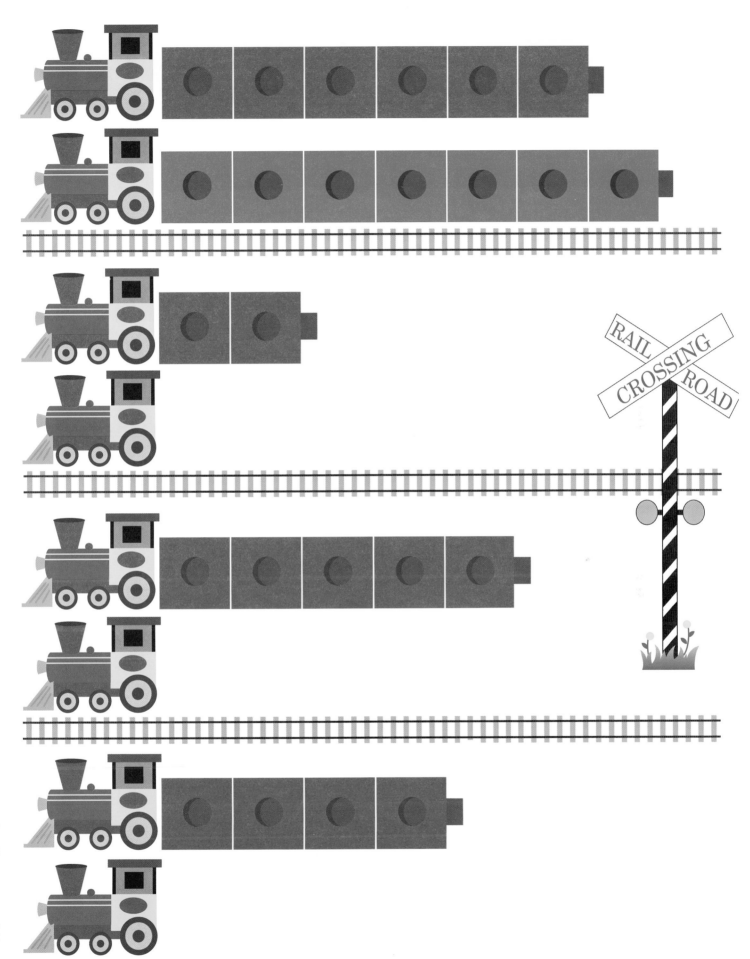

Use connecting cubes to make a train that is longer than the red train. Then draw a line to show how long the train is that you made.

Home Note: Encourage your child to make a block train or a clay "snake." Then have your child make one longer and one shorter.

191

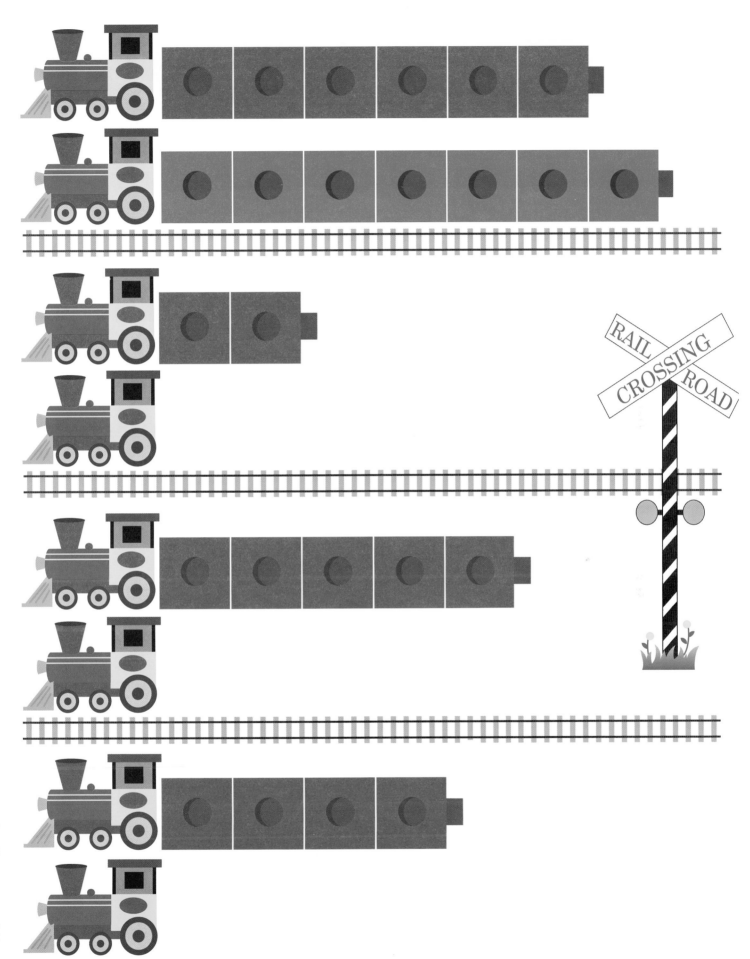

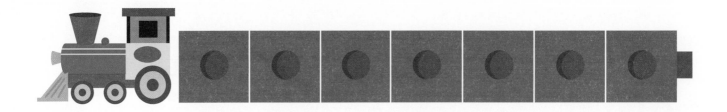

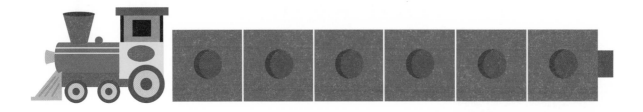

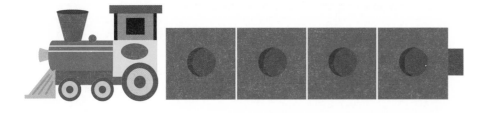

Draw a line above the cube train to make a
shorter train. Draw a line below the cube train
to make a longer train.

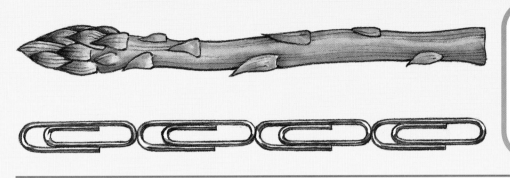
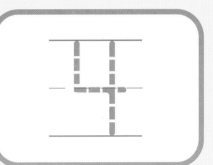

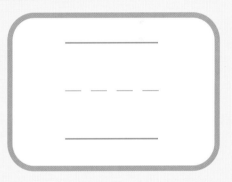

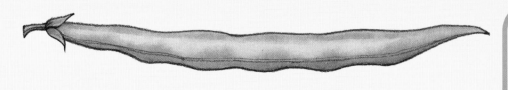

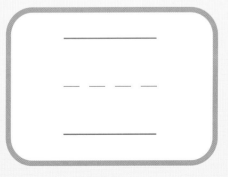

Use paperclips to measure each object.
Write the number that tells how long.

Home Note: Encourage your child to use nonstandard units such as paper clips to measure the lengths of various small objects.

193

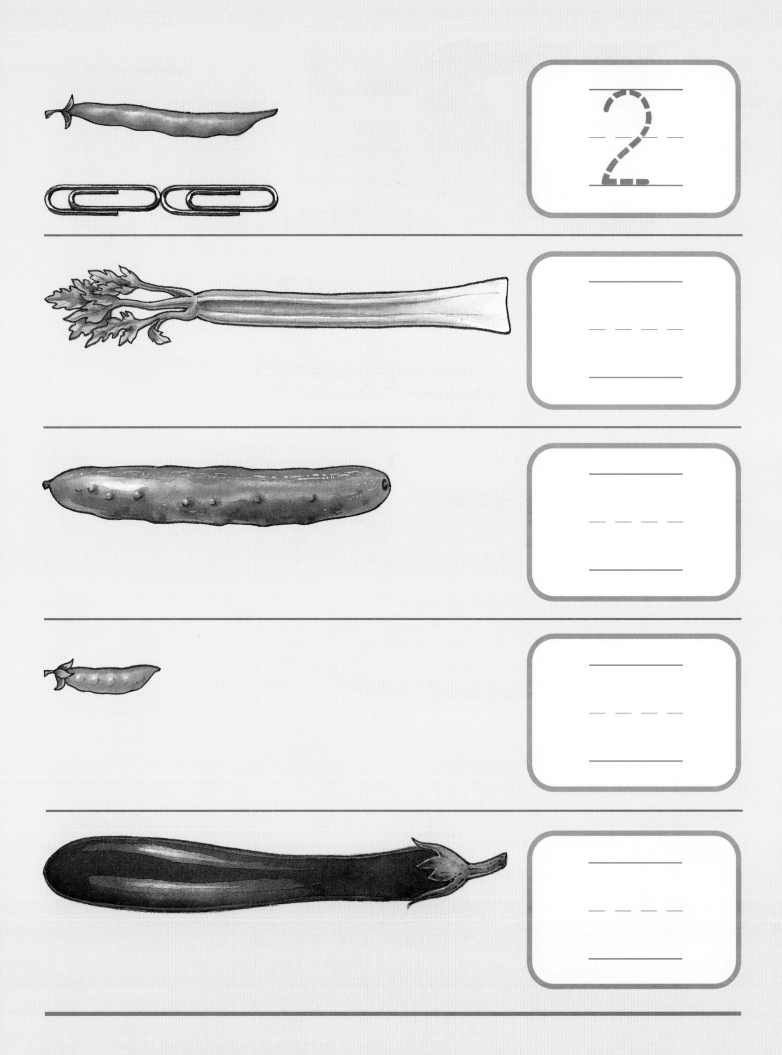

Measure each object using paper clips. Write how many paper clips long.

Estimate   ## Measure

_ _ _ _ _ _ _   _ _ _ _ _ _ _

_____   _____

Estimate   ## Measure

_ _ _ _ _ _ _   _ _ _ _ _ _ _

_____   _____

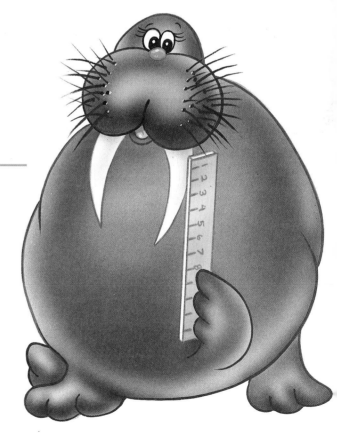

Estimate   ## Measure

_ _ _ _ _ _ _   _ _ _ _ _ _ _

_____   _____

Estimate how many strips long and write the number on the red line. Then use punch-out strips to measure. Paste the strips below the object. Write how many strips on the blue line.

Home Note: Encourage your child to estimate how many units long an object is. Then help your child measure the object and compare the measurement with the estimate.

195

Estimate

Measure

_ _ _ _ _ _   _ _ _ _ _ _

Estimate

Measure

_ _ _ _ _ _   _ _ _ _ _ _

Estimate

Measure

_ _ _ _ _ _   _ _ _ _ _ _

196   Estimate how many strips long and write the
number on the red line. Then use punch-out
strips to measure. Paste the strips below the
object. Write how many strips on the blue line.

Name _____

Use punch-out bushes to show where you want to plant them. Use a crayon to draw a fence around the bushes. Count and write how many pieces of fence are needed.

Home Note: Encourage your child to use units such as paper clips to measure the distance around objects.

How Far Is It?

Count how many units there are between animals. Write the number.

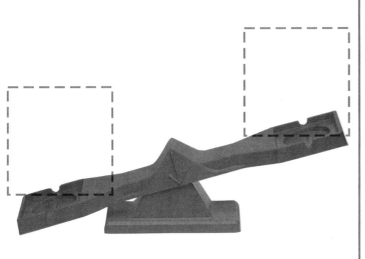

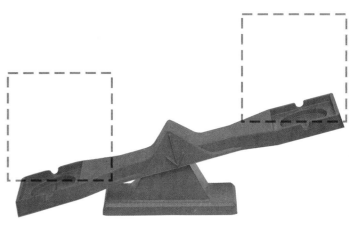

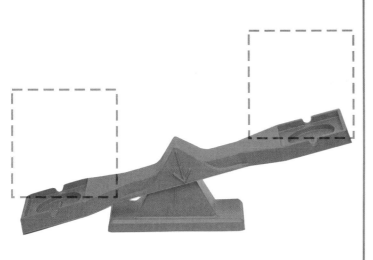

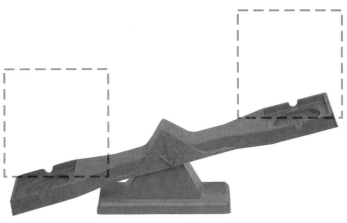

Find these objects in your classroom. Weigh any two objects on a balance scale. Place the cutouts on your page to show how your scale looked. Then paste.

Home Note: Encourage your child to guess which of two household objects is heavier or lighter. Then have your child check by picking up or weighing the objects.

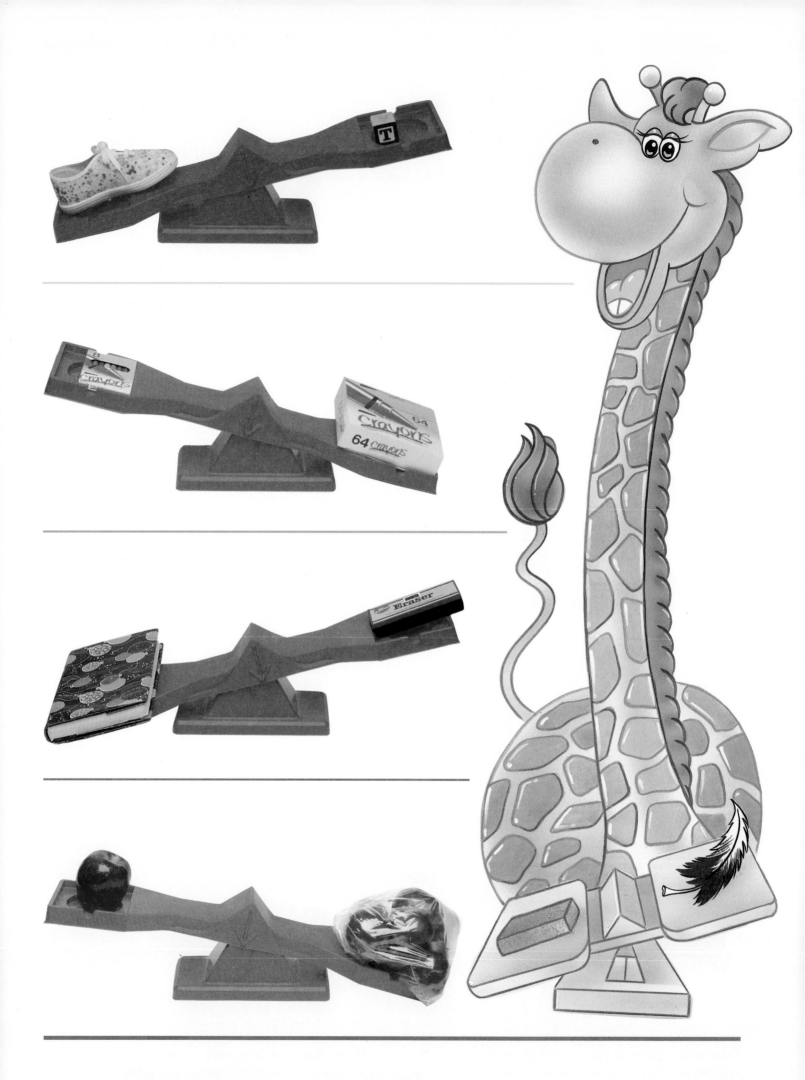

Ring the object that is heavier. Draw X on the object that is lighter.

Use cutouts to put a container on the left that holds less. Put a container on the right that holds more. Paste.

Home Note: Encourage your child to guess which of two containers holds more or less. Then have your child check by pouring water from one container to the other.

201

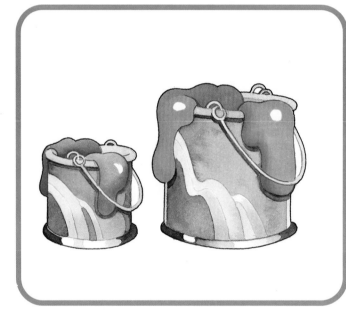

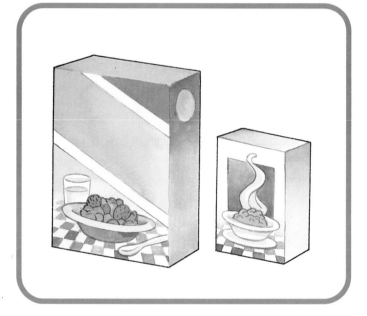

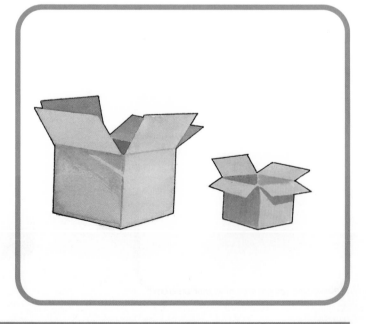

Ring the container that holds more. Draw X
on the container that holds less.

	Estimate	**Measure**
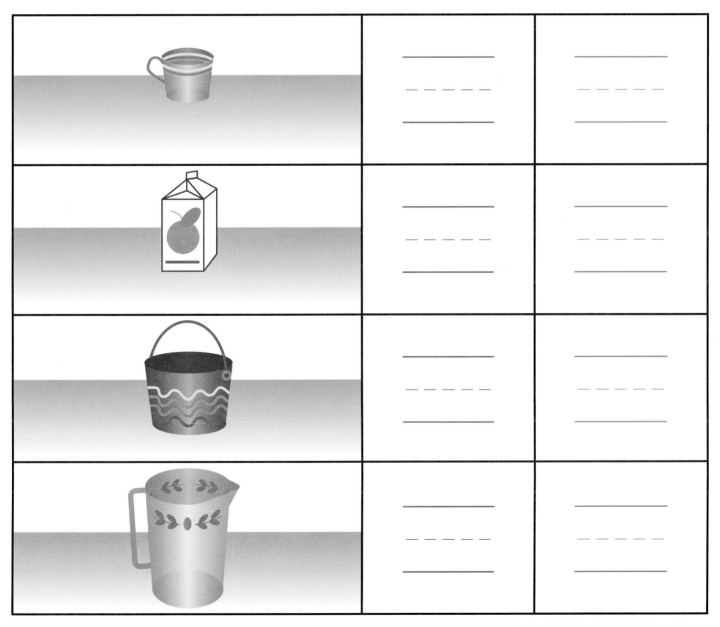	_____	_____
	_____	_____
	_____	_____
	_____	_____

Estimate how many cups are needed to fill each container. Write the number. Then measure how many and write the number.

Home Note: Encourage your child to compare a cup measure to a quart measure and estimate about how many times he or she would have to pour the contents into the other to fill it.

203

Chapter Review/Test

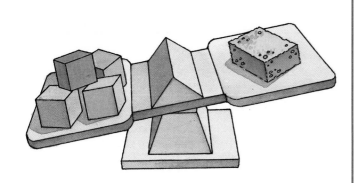

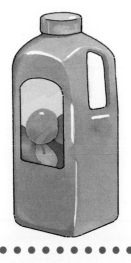

Top: Count how many paper clips to measure the length of the string.
Write the number. Draw a string that is shorter. **Middle:** Ring the heavier
object on each scale. **Bottom:** Draw X on each container that holds less.

204

Which Weighs Less?

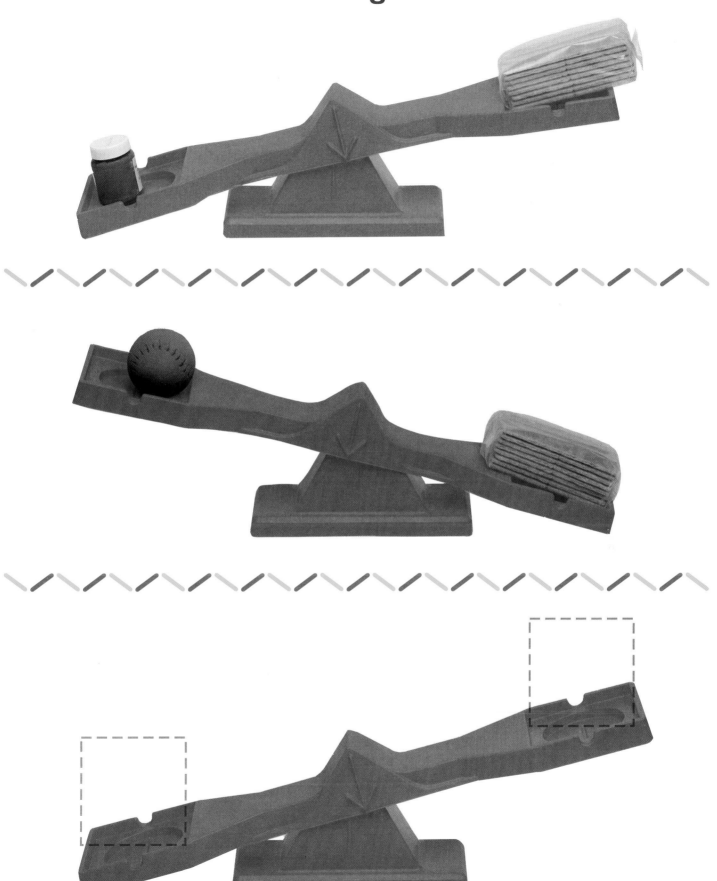

Look at the scales on the page. Think about the pictures. Then place the jar and the ball on the scale to show which is lighter. Paste.

Home Note: Encourage your child to compare the weights of two objects and then compare the weights of several objects.

205

Which Weighs More?

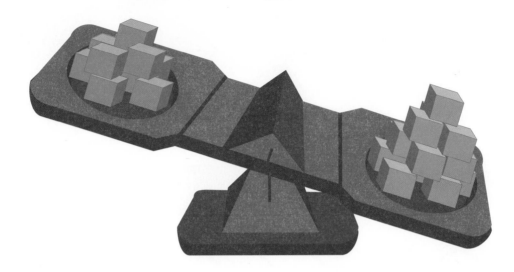

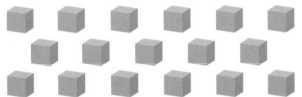

(17)

10

12

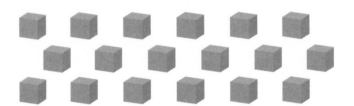

18

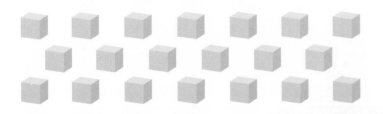

20

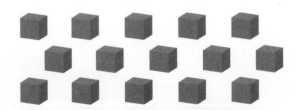

15

Use cubes to make groups. Put each group
on a different side of the scale. Ring the
number that tells which group has more.

My Little Math Book

by _____

Home Note: Your child may enjoy reading this book to you. You may wish to discuss the different ways of measuring shown.

1

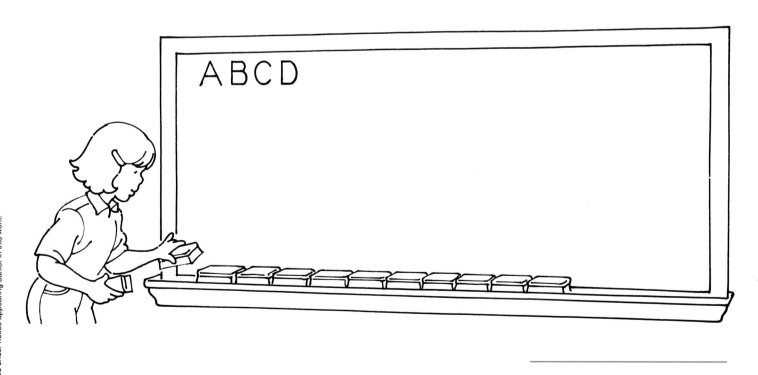

ABCD

_____

_ _ _ _ _ _ _ _

_____

Guess how many erasers are needed to measure the chalkboard. Write the number.

3

2   About how many feet away are the cones?

4   Ring the object that weighs more.

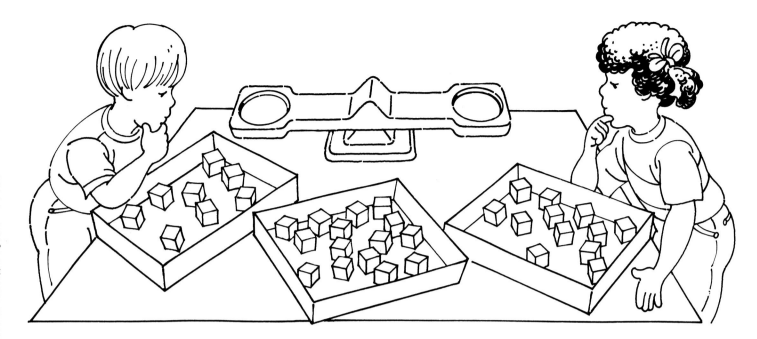

Ring the box that weighs less .

5

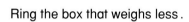

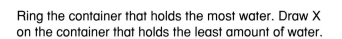

Ring the container that holds the most water. Draw X
on the container that holds the least amount of water.

7

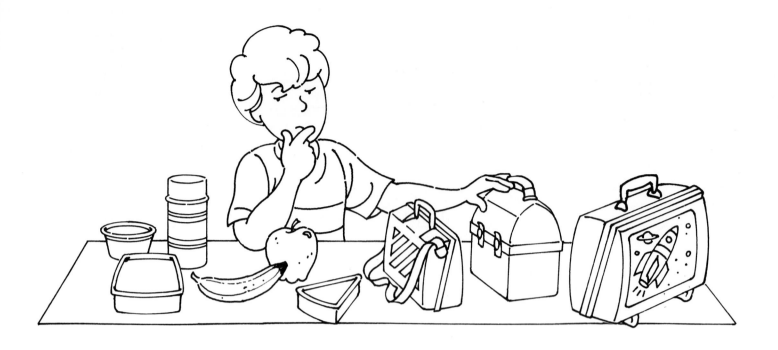

6   Ring the lunch box that will hold the lunch.

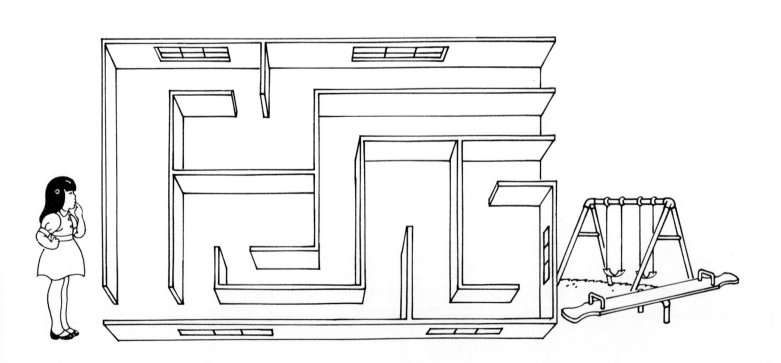

8   Color the shortest path to the playground.

Joining and Separating

STORY TIME

Listen to the story.
"The Farmer's Eggs"

School-Home Connection

Dear Family,
   We started a new chapter in our math book today. We will be learning about addition and subtraction. Here is a game for us to play together at home.

                    Love,
                    Your child

Sharing and Doing

Give or Take

To play this game, copy the cards below and use 20 counters or small objects such as buttons, paper clips, or toothpicks for each player. Cut out the cards, shuffle them, and place them facedown in a pile. Each player begins with four counters. Put the remaining counters in a group in the center of the table. Taking turns, players draw a card.

When players draw a − 1 card, they take one counter from their group and put it in the group in the center. When players draw a + 1 card, they take a counter from the group in the center and add it to their group. After each turn, the player says how many counters he or she has. The first player with ten counters wins the game.

+ 1	+ 1	+ 1	+ 1	+ 1	+ 1
+ 1	− 1	+ 1	− 1	+ 1	− 1
+ 1	− 1	+ 1	− 1	+ 1	− 1

Use after page 226.

Listen to the story. Use punchouts to act out the story. Write how many in all. Paste.

Home Note: Encourage your child to tell a story about each picture.

Tell a story about each picture. Put a counter on each cow. Count. Write how many in all.

Tell a story about each picture. Use counters to act out the story. Write how many in each group. Then join the groups. Write how many in all.

Home Note: Encourage your child to draw a picture that shows the joining of groups.

211

2   2   4

1   1   ___

3   3   ___

Tell a story about each picture. Use counters to act out the story. Write how many in each group. Then join the groups. Write how many in all.

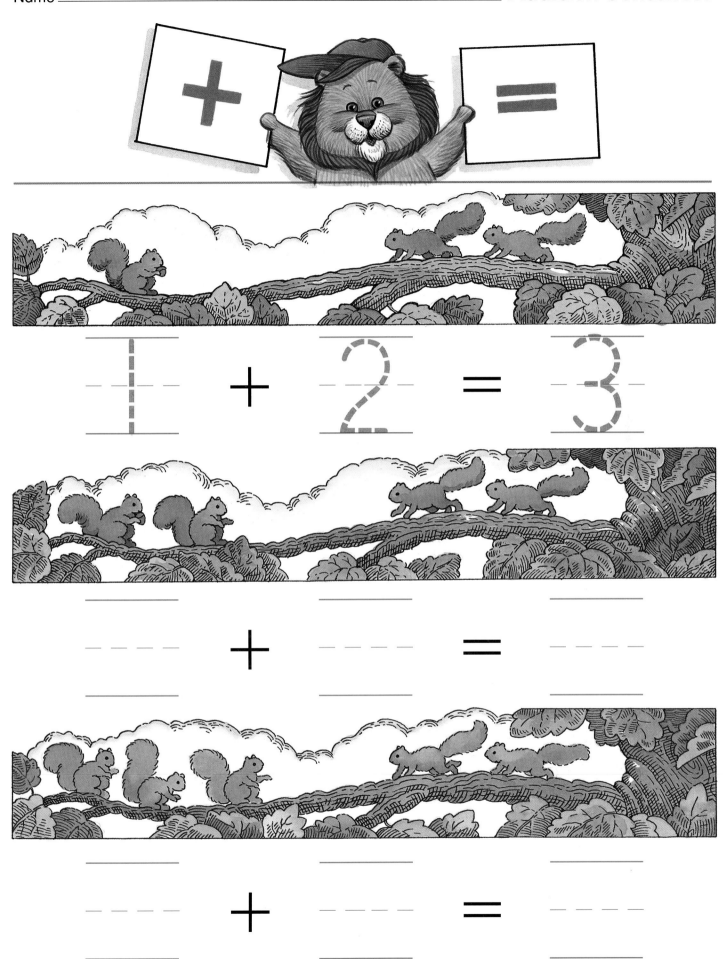

1 + 2 = 3

____ + ____ = ____

____ + ____ = ____

Tell a story about each picture. Use counters to act out each story. Write the addition sentence that tells the story.

Home Note: Encourage your child to draw a picture that shows the joining of groups and to write an addition sentence telling what happened.

213

$$4 + 2 = 6$$

____ + ____ = ____

____ + ____ = ____

Tell a story about each picture. Use counters
to act out the story. Write the addition
sentence that tells the story.

Workmat

1+1=2 2+1=3   3+1=4   4+1=5

1 + 1 = 2

___ + 1 = ___

___ + 1 = ___

Tell a story about each picture. Use a workmat and counters to act out the story. Write the addition sentence that tells the story.

Home Note: Tell your child a story about an addition situation. Encourage your child to use objects to act out each story.

215

3 + 1 = 4

1 + 1 =

4 + 1 =

5 + 1 =

1 + 1 =

2 + 1 =

Count the apples in each tree. Draw 1 more.
Add. Write how many in all.

Workmat

$$4¢ + 1¢ = 5¢$$

$$\_\_¢ + \_\_¢ = \_\_¢$$

$$\_\_¢ + \_\_¢ = \_\_¢$$

Use a workmat and pennies.
Count. Write the addition sentence.
Write how much money in all.

Home Note: Encourage your child to show
you what money was needed to buy the toys.
You may wish to let your child use real coins.

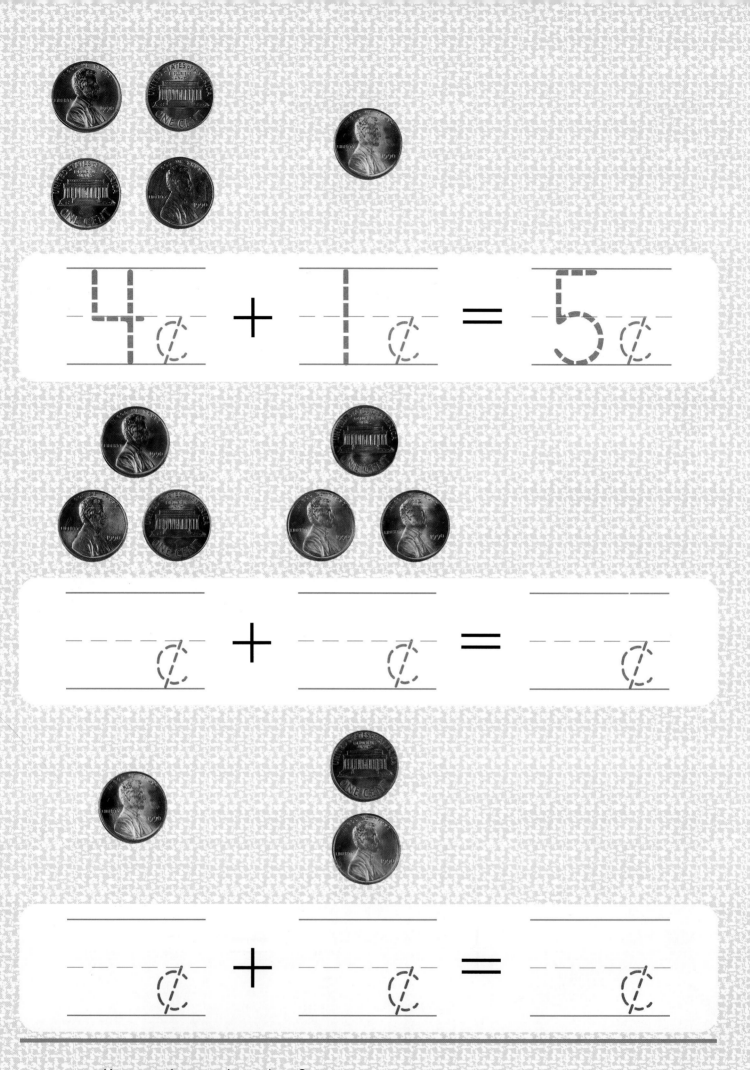

$$4¢ + 1¢ = 5¢$$

$$\underline{\hspace{2cm}}¢ + \underline{\hspace{2cm}}¢ = \underline{\hspace{2cm}}¢$$

$$\underline{\hspace{2cm}}¢ + \underline{\hspace{2cm}}¢ = \underline{\hspace{2cm}}¢$$

Use a workmat and pennies. Count.
Write the addition sentence that tells how
much money in all.

Name _____

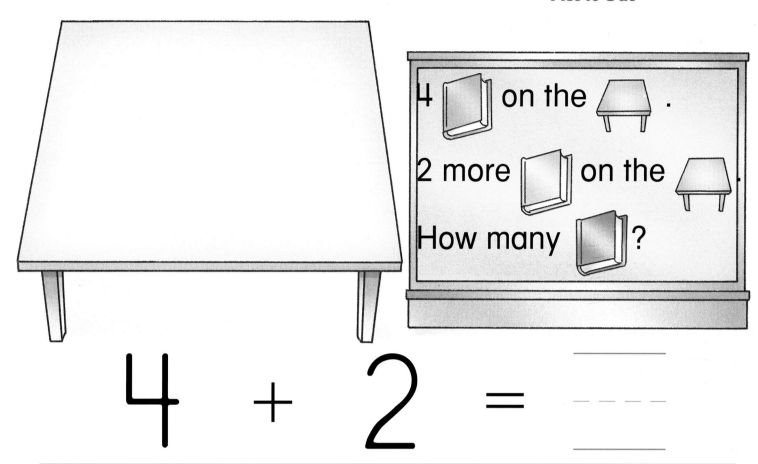

4 [book] on the [table].

2 more [book] on the [table].

How many [book] ?

$$4 \quad + \quad 2 \quad = \quad \underline{\quad\quad}$$

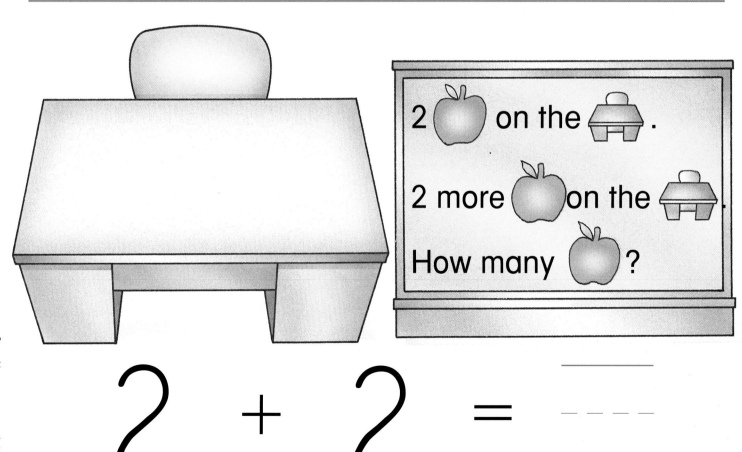

2 [apple] on the [desk].

2 more [apple] on the [desk].

How many [apple] ?

$$2 \quad + \quad 2 \quad = \quad \underline{\quad\quad}$$

Read the story and act it out. Add.
Write how many. Then draw a picture.

Home Note: Make up an addition story about objects in the home. Encourage your child to act out the story.

219

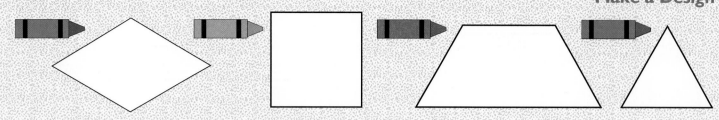

Color inside the shapes as shown.

3

Listen to the story. Use your ducks to act out the story. Count how many ducks in all. Then move some away to show the ducks leaving. Write how many ducks are left.

Home Note: Encourage your child to tell a story about each picture and use objects to act it out.

221

Listen to the story. Use counters to act out the story.
Put a counter on each horse. Count how many horses
in all. Then move some away to show the horses
leaving. Write how many horses are left.

Name _____

More Subtraction

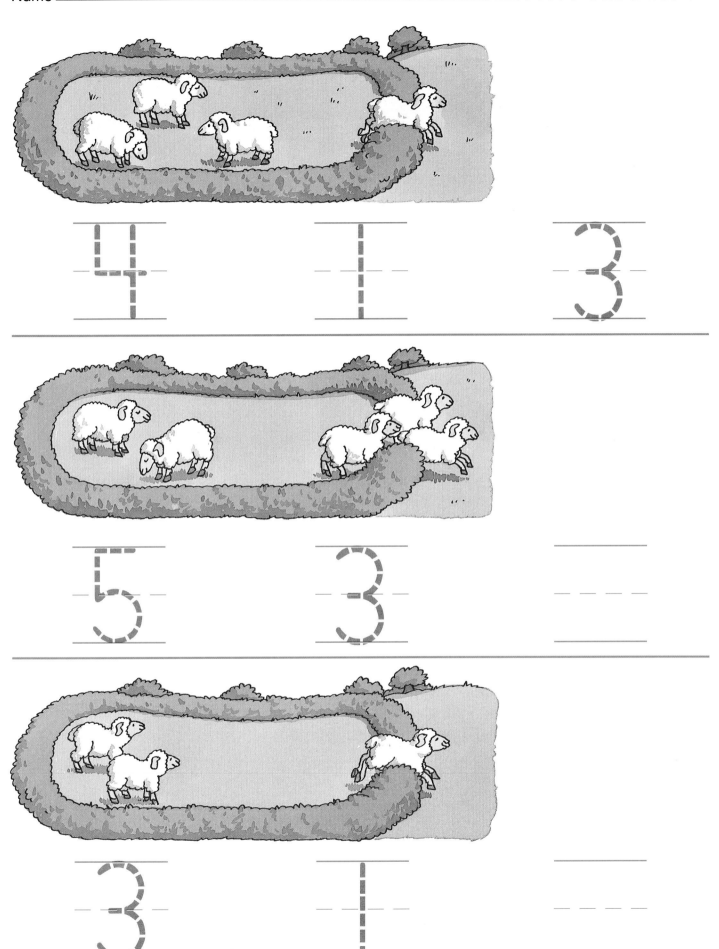

4   1   3

5   3   ___

3   1   ___

Use counters to act out the story. Put a counter on each animal. Count how many in all. Then move some away to show the animals leaving. Count how many are left. Write the numbers.

Home Note: Encourage your child to tell you a subtraction story for each set of pictures. You may wish to have your child use objects to act out each story.

223

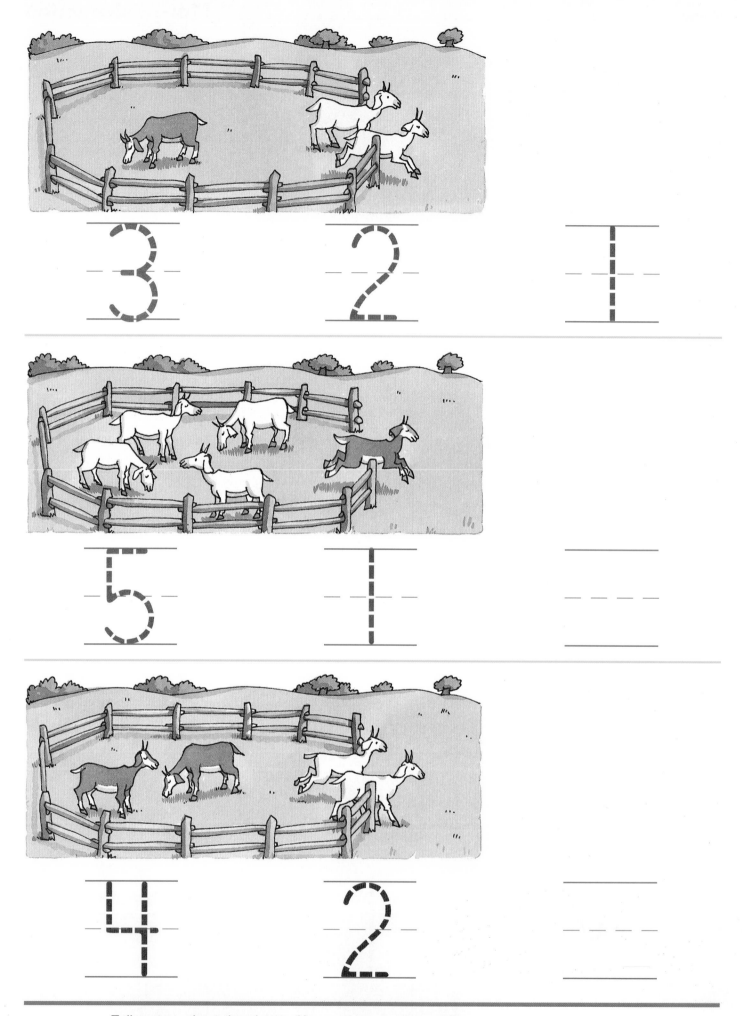

3   2   1

5   1   ___

4   2   ___

Tell a story about the picture. Use counters to act out the
story. Put a counter on each animal. Count how many in all.
Then move some away to show the animals leaving. Count
how many are left. Write the numbers.

224

$$3 - 2 = 1$$

_____ _____ _____

_____ — _____ = _____

_____ _____ _____

_____ — _____ = _____

Use counters to act out the story. Put a counter on each animal. Count how many in all. Then move some away to show the animals leaving. Count how many are left. Write the number sentence.

Home Note: Encourage your child to tell a subtraction story about each picture and to read the subtraction sentence that also tells the story.

225

$$5 - 3 = 2$$

___ ___ ___

___ — ___ = ___

___ ___ ___

___ ___ ___

___ — ___ = ___

___ ___ ___

Tell a subtraction story about each group of pictures. Use counters to act out the story. Put a counter on each animal. Then move some away to show the animals leaving. Count how many are left. Write the number sentence.

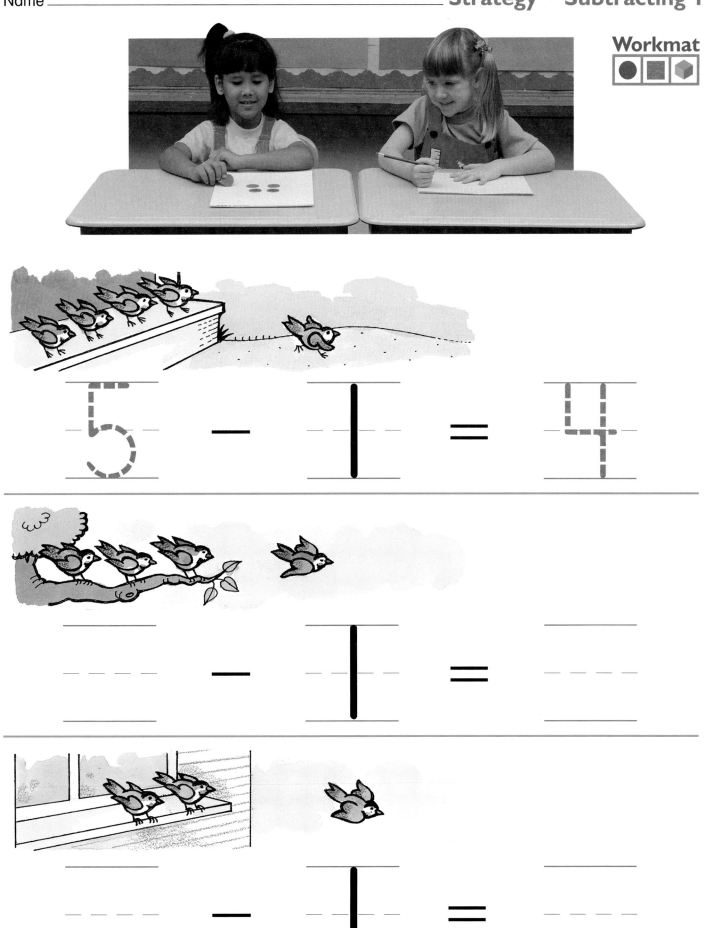

Workmat

$$5 - 1 = 4$$

Tell a subtraction story about each picture.
Use a workmat and counters to act out
each story. Write the subtraction sentence
that tells the story.

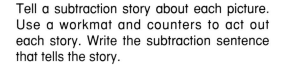

Home Note: Encourage your child to tell a
subtraction story about each picture.

227

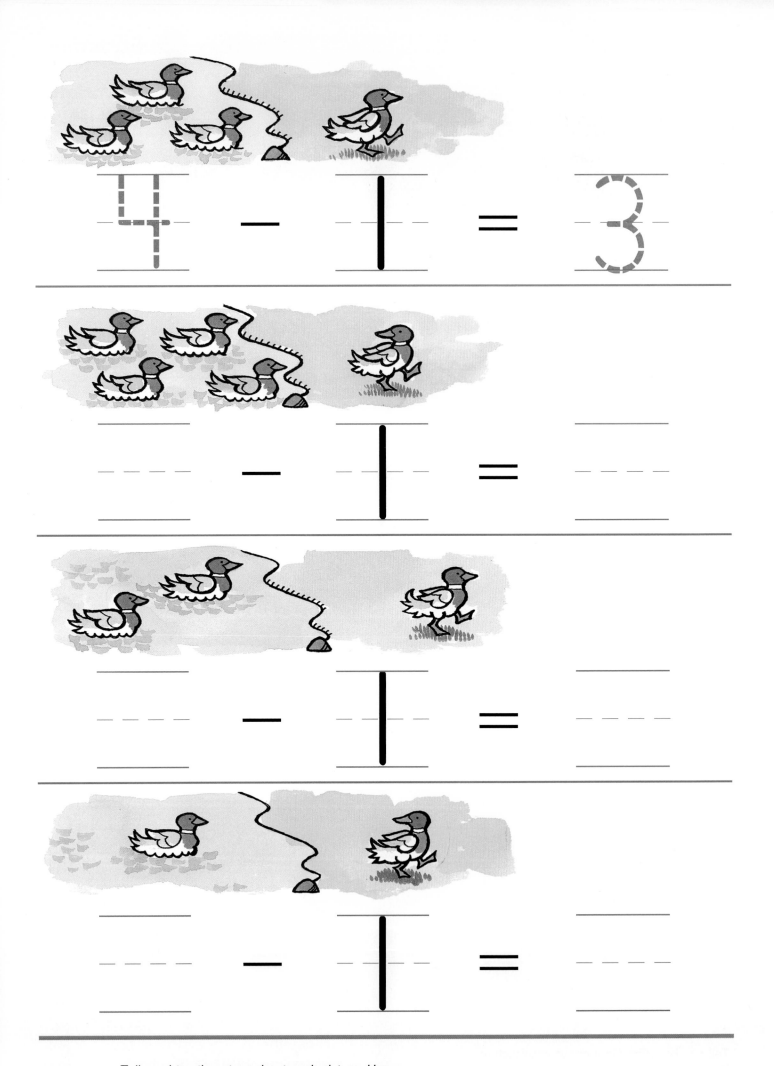

4 − 1 = 3

___ − 1 = ___

___ − 1 = ___

___ − 1 = ___

Tell a subtraction story about each picture. Use a
workmat and counters to act out the story. Write
the subtraction sentence that tells the story.

Subtracting Money

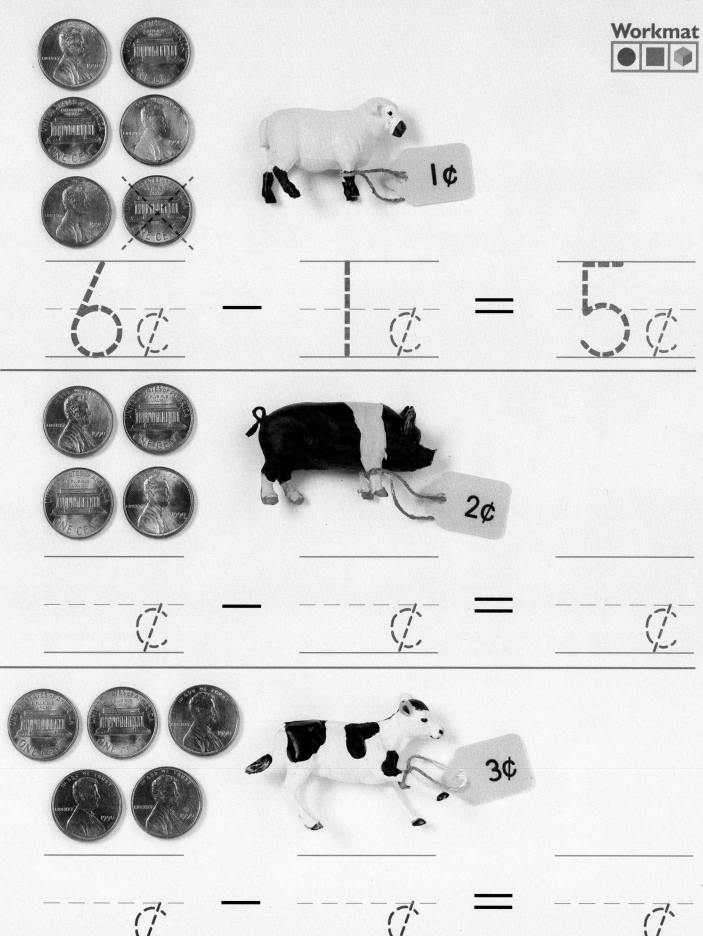

$$6¢ - 1¢ = 5¢$$

$$\_\_¢ - \_\_¢ = \_\_¢$$

$$\_\_¢ - \_\_¢ = \_\_¢$$

Use pennies and a workmat to act out each story. Cross out the pennies you need to buy the toy. Write the number sentence.

Home Note: Encourage your child to use real pennies to retell each story.

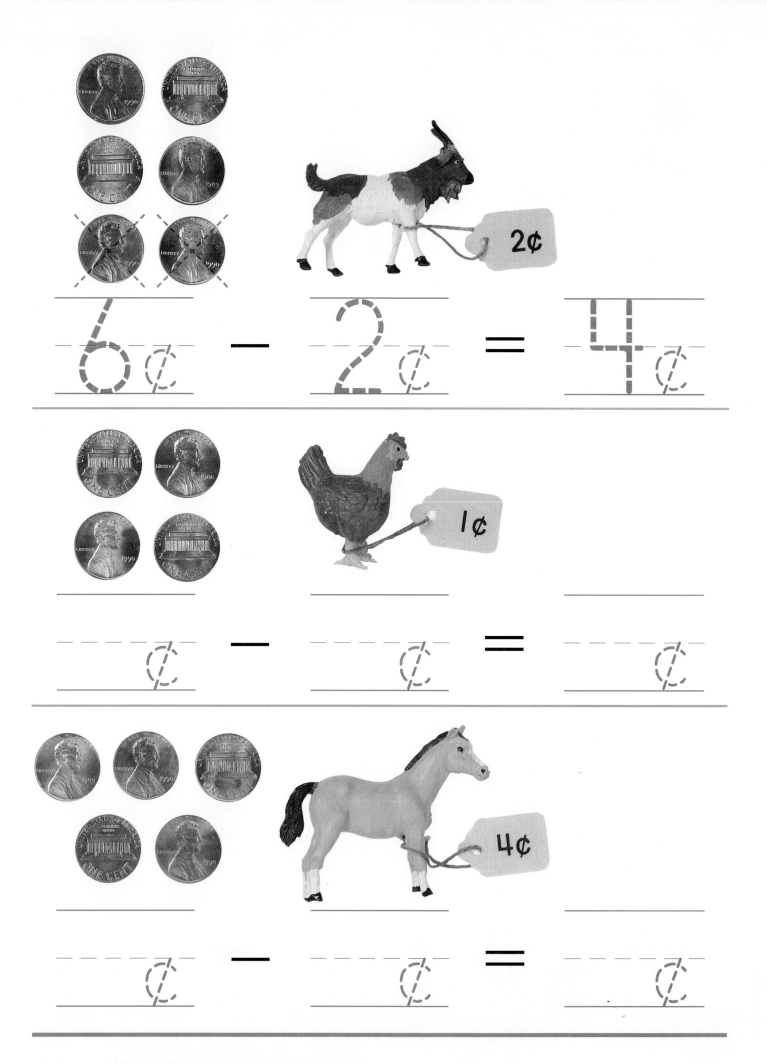

$$6\cent - 2\cent = 4\cent$$

$$\underline{}\cent - \underline{}\cent = \underline{}\cent$$

$$\underline{}\cent - \underline{}\cent = \underline{}\cent$$

230 Use pennies and a workmat to act out each story. Cross out the pennies you need to buy the toy. Write the number sentence.

$3 + 1 = 4$ $(3 - 1 = 2)$

$2 + 1 = 3$ $2 - 1 = 1$

Tell a story about each picture. Ring the number sentence that tells what happened in each picture.

Home Note: Make up some addition and subtraction stories. Encourage your child to tell whether each story is about addition or subtraction.

231

4 + 1 = 5   4 − 1 = 3

5 + 1 = 6   5 − 1 = 4

Tell a story about each picture. Ring the
number sentence that tells what happened in
each picture.

232

Name _____

_____

- -

_____

Tell a story about each picture. Write a number sentence. Press the number sentence on your calculator. Write the answer.

Home Note: Encourage your child to create addition and subtraction stories and to use a calculator to show the number sentence.

233

 ON/C 4 + 2 =

 ON/C 2 − 1 =

Tell a story about each picture. Write a
number sentence. Press the number sentence
on your calculator. Write the answer.

1 + 1 = ____					
2 + 1 = ____					
3 + 1 = ____					
4 + 1 = ____					
5 + 1 = ____					

Use cubes to model addition sentences.
Count. Finish the addition sentences.
Then remove the cubes and color.

Home Note: Encourage your child to point
out the patterns in the blocks and numbers.
You may wish to have your child try to extend
the patterns.

235

Chapter Review/Test

_____   _____   _____

_ _ _ _ _   **+**   _ _ _ _ _   **=**   _ _ _ _ _

_____   _____   _____

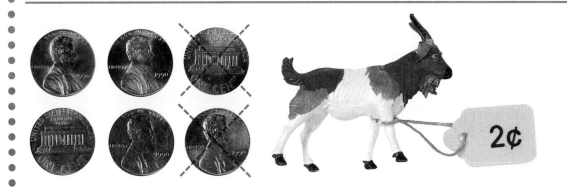

_____   _____   _____

¢   **—**   ¢   **=**   ¢

$$3 + 1 = 4 \qquad 3 - 1 = 2$$

Top and Middle: Listen to the story about the pictures. Use counters to act out each story. Write the numbers. **Bottom:** Ring the number sentence that tells the story.

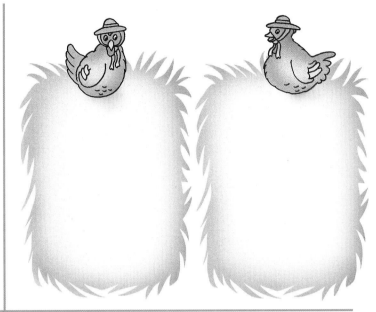

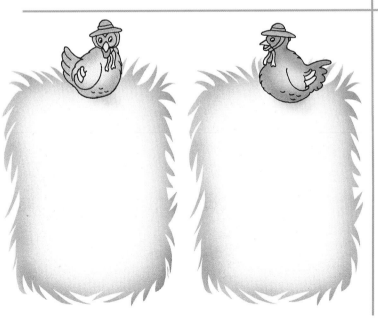
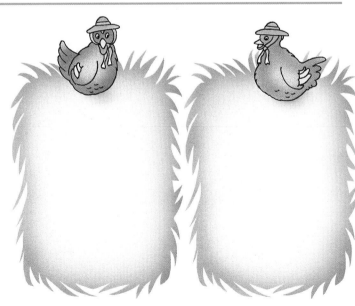

Put counters in the nests to show different ways that a group of six can be made. Remove the counters and draw eggs in the nests. Then make another group of six.

Home Note: Collect small objects, and encourage your child to group them in different combinations of the same number.

237

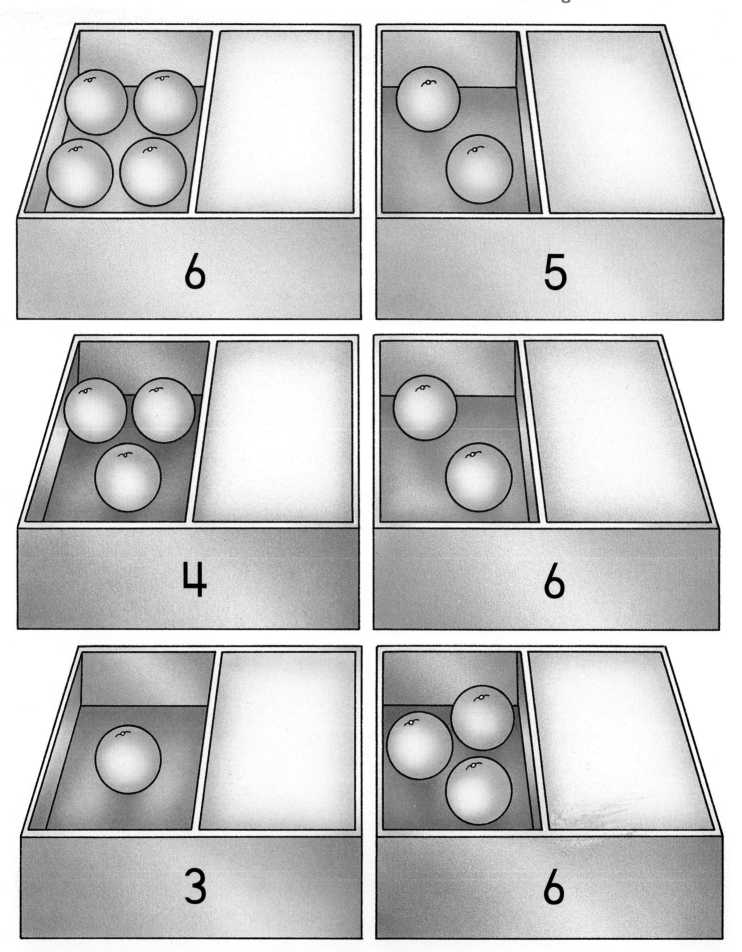

6

5

4

6

3

6

The number tells how many oranges in all go
in the box. Draw the oranges needed to show
that number of oranges in the box in all.

My Little Math Book

by _____

Home Note: Your child may enjoy reading this book to you. You may wish to encourage your child to tell more addition and subtraction stories.

1

$$\text{\_\_\_\_} + \text{\_\_\_\_} = \text{\_\_\_\_}$$

Write a number sentence to tell the addition story.

3

2

_____ + _____ = _____

4   Write a number sentence to tell the addition story.

5

_____ — _____ = _____

Write a number sentence to tell the subtraction story.

7

_____ _____ _____

----- **—** ----- **=** -----

_____ _____ _____

6   Write a number sentence to tell the subtraction story.

$4 - 1 = 3$

$2 + 1 = 3$

8   Draw a line from each picture to the number sentence it matches.

Shapes

ball

box

can

cone

circle

square

rectangle

triangle

Money

penny	nickel	dime
1¢ 1¢	5¢ 5¢	10¢ 10¢

Comparing Numbers

same	more	fewer

Top, Middle, Bottom

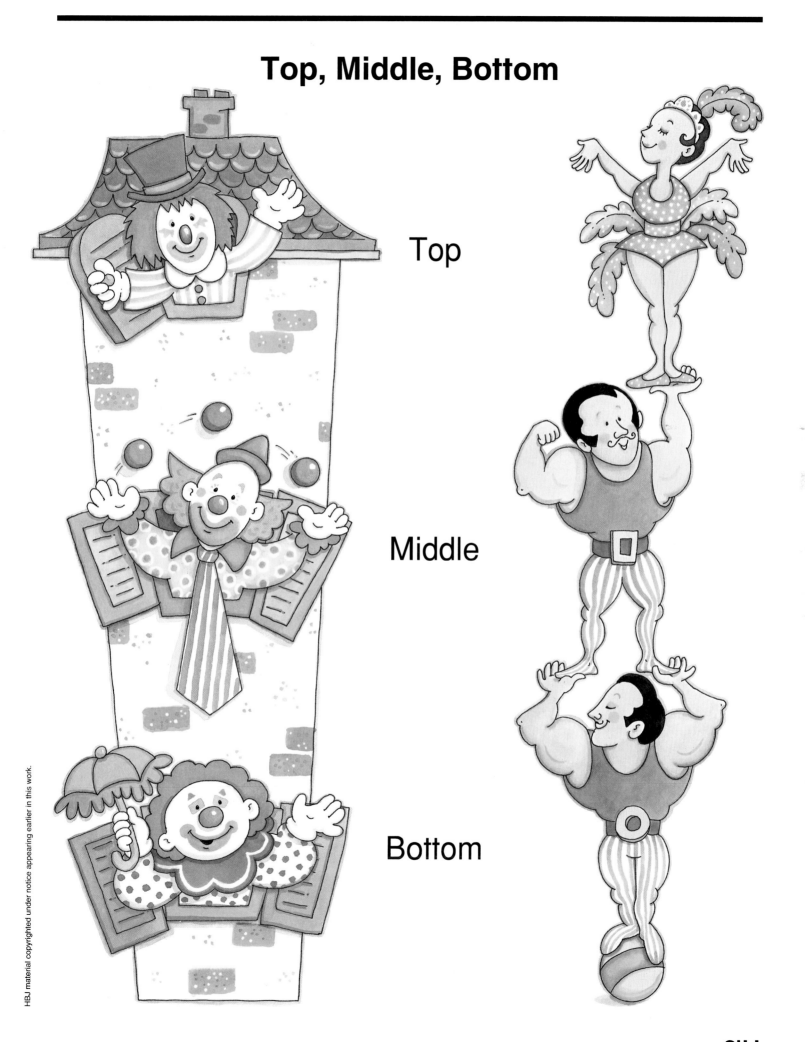

Top

Middle

Bottom

Before, After, Between

Before   Between   After

Above and Below

Above

Below

Left and Right

left 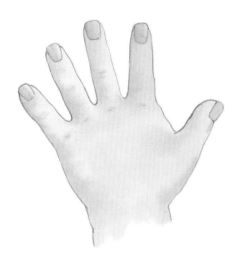 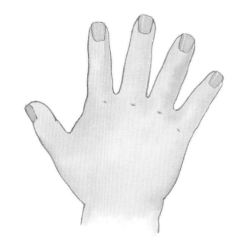 right

left   right

left  right

Same and Different

Same

Different

Same Size

Different Size

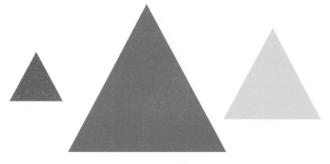

Same Shape

Different Shape

Same Color

Different Color

Long and Short

Long			Short	
Longer			Shorter	
Longest			Shortest	

Short and Tall

Shorter			Shorter	
Longer			Longer	

Short   Shorter   Shortest

Tall   Taller   Tallest

Numbers 0 to 10

0		zero
1		one
2		two
3		three
4		four
5		five
6		six
7		seven
8		eight
9		nine
10		ten

Ordinal Numbers

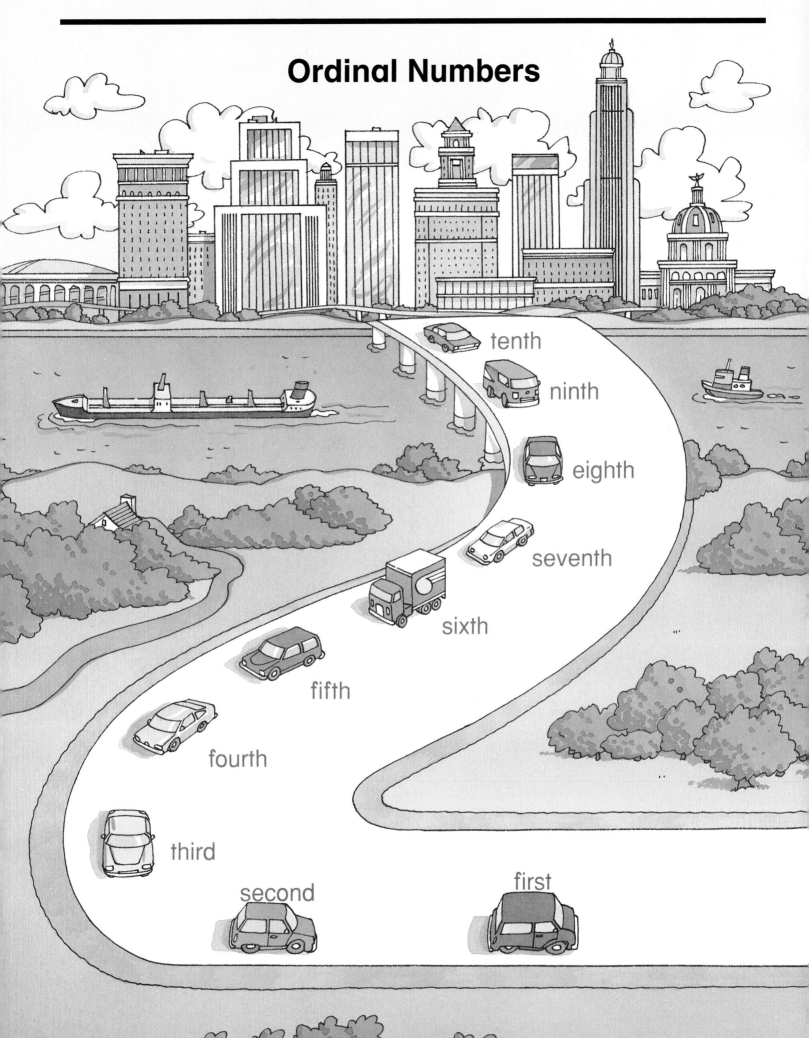

tenth

ninth

eighth

seventh

sixth

fifth

fourth

third

second

first

Time

hour

4 o'clock

4:00

Addition

4 + 1 = 5

4 + 2 = 6

3 + 2 = 5

Subtraction

6   –   3   =   3

4   –   1   =   3

3   –   1   =   2

Page 5

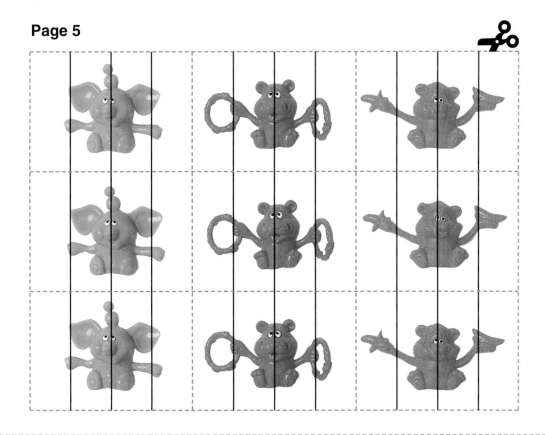

Page 23

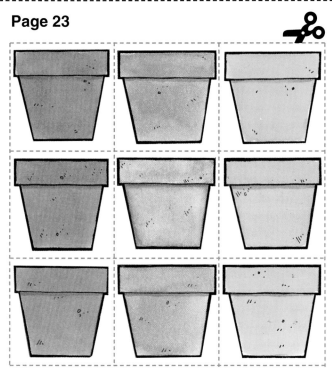

Page 27

251

Page 28

Page 102

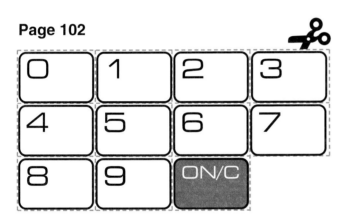

Page 114

Page 177

Page 182

Page 183

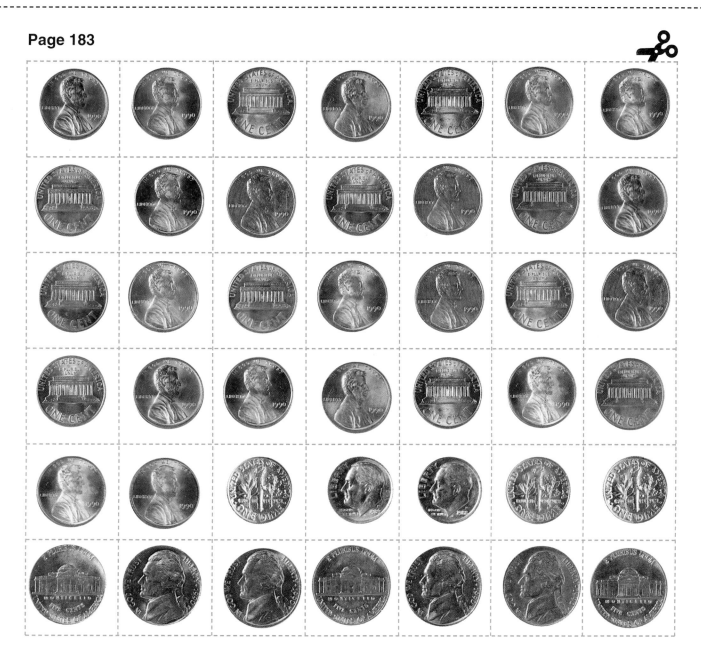

Page 199

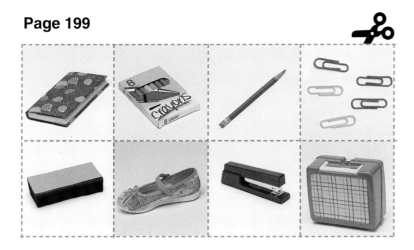

Page 201

Page 205

Page 3

Page 9

Page 7

Page 25

Page 31

Page 37